MW00341171

The Me I Was

The true story of how death by motorcycle gave me life.

Jaclyn Lanae

Published in 2015
Shelter50 Publishing Collective
Rapid City, South Dakota, USA

For commercial purposes please contact:
Shelter50publishingcollective@gmail.com
www.shelter50publishingcollective.com

© 2015 Shelter50 Publishing Collective

Credit for re-use is appreciated. Who knows who owns what when it comes to words anyway. Unless you're a major corporation and want to patent the rain, give credit where credit is due :)

First Edition

Printed and bound in the United States of America

Cover & Book design by Bonny Fleming and Jaclyn Kennison
www.BonzeyePhotography.com

ISBN: **0986249521**
ISBN 13: **978-0986249525**

To my Jess… If only all the world could have a heart as big as yours. You are my most treasured friend.

To my Todd… Never in my wildest dreams did I imagine someone so magical would walk this road with me, holding my hand. Even carrying me sometimes. My heart is forever yours.

To my mother and father… I am literally here today because of you – several times over. I love you more than I could ever say.

To every blessed soul who prayed for me, cared for me, supported me, and believed in me…

Thank you.

FOREWARD

When I first met Jaci I couldn't escape that rare feeling of dejavu. A mutual friend of ours thought we should meet recognizing that she had a most extraordinary story that was undoubtedly important to share. He knew that I would find in her not only a kindred spirit, but a sensitive soul who had been putting pen to paper over time to give meaning to an event in her life that nearly shattered it and left her for dead on the side of a road.

We are both survivors of unusual life altering catastrophes and rather than simply pick ourselves up and move on, our natures demanded reason. I was transfixed as she began to weave together the circumstances of a day in her life, the details that surrounded a seemingly ordinary one. How she loved nothing more than the anticipation of another motorcycle rally, her own love of riding that brought her into a world where all was heightened by the sound of your engine coming to life beneath you, nothing to hold you back but your own ability and skill to maneuver the next turn. To feel the glorious ineffable freedom that lifts the hair from the back of your neck and lets you feel power and joy with the people who are real brothers and sisters, who have your back. This is a world Jaci navigated with well won respect. I was spellbound.

This is your invitation to take a ride, a real ride through her beloved Black Hills and mine, on the back of her motorcycle as the wind fans her face, the road leads the way out and over landscapes of laughter and fearlessness with a cavalcade of comrades who will show her much magic and perhaps some sleight of hand along the way. She will traverse new vistas looking for the answers that elude her and some that work for a while when, one beautiful day with all her dreams tucked securely in her back pocket, floating through the canyon on a cloudless wave, safe as a bird in flight on her beloved bike she inexplicitly falls. The music is over. Dead silence. The world stops spinning…. Mortality… Morphine… Terror… The end?

Jaci takes us on a journey of discovery that is conversely unique to each of us, yet connects us universally as human beings, to remind us that we are significantly more than we realize. Ironically, fittingly communal arrival is a place that simply is. Come. What happens next is revelation, awakening. It is raw, bold, and pure. It is a mystery unfolded and gracefully told. It asks nothing less than seeking beyond the puny limits of mere survival to reaching the unexplored depths to uncover the answers to the very core of who and what we are and why we are here. Read on. Unwrap the beauty revealed within. You will be glad you did.

~Merlyn Magner, author of *Come Into the Water*

Life is a series of experiences. Extract the lessons, hold them in your heart, and let the rest of it go. Set it down and walk away like abandoning luggage in the airport. Struggle and challenges are only baggage if you carry them around with you.

~Jaclyn Lanae

ACKNOWLEDGMENTS.

Often when people hear the story you hold in your hands for the first time, they respond with their own tale of transformation, and often that story begins with "Well, it was nothing like what you experienced, but…" Please don't do that. These kinds of things can't be compared. Our worst pain is only as bad as the worst pain we've ever felt, our greatest joy is only as good as the greatest joy we've ever experienced. There is no comparison, no better or worse.

I wrote this story because I had to. It was therapeutic, really, at least to begin with. Eventually, I realized I liked to tell the tale… not because it was a particularly lovely story, but because of the particularly beautiful things I learned, the particularly beautiful appreciation for life I was given.

We've *all* been through and survived incredible things. We're *all* brave because we keep going, keep believing, keep hoping. Even after our hearts get broken, we keep loving, and that is maybe the bravest thing of all.

ONE

The thunder of motorcycles was in my ears and the air stunk of leather and sweat and the smoke of the cigarette pinched between my fingers. I'd found relief from the early August sun on the cool iron stairs in the shade of a building I had come to call my home away from home.

Four hundred fifty thousand bikers had done the same, for the one-week each year when the Black Hills of South Dakota become legendary. They gathered here, a celebration of the machine, the experience, and the lifestyle. For many, it was temporary. For me it had become – in part – a definition.

As the thin paper sizzled in surrender to the stoking cherry, my eyes wandered over the scene before me. Rows and rows of bikers between rows and rows of tents bathed the asphalt parking lot like a giant flag - to me, a fluttering banner of possibility.

A too-quick marriage had fallen through two years after its inception and I had found myself living with my parents, too old to be there and too broke to do anything about it. When I had asked my husband to move back to his hometown I had hit rock bottom and was scraping deep gouges in the muck. The motorcycle dealership had been like a strong and fatherly hand reaching down to pull me from the dark abyss.

It was a rather small business - save for Rally Week - and the staff was like family, the regular customers like favorite cousins. I felt a part of it, and as though I had something to offer, something that was appreciated. Within those walls I had found friendship and hope, a sense of value.

Over the last few years I had built something resembling a normal life. I had found a wonderful downtown apartment, bought myself a car, stuffed a social calendar and began to pay off the old debts my younger self and her husband had acquired. I felt like my life was starting to look like it should. I was finally standing on my own again, and was able to hold my head up.

Big rigs painted with the logos of famous and not-yet-famous bike builders squatted in a long row, basking in the sun across from me, clusters of riders clad largely in black milling about the machines. From my seat I could see them turning their heads slowly, running their eyes over the graceful curves and smooth lines, admiring the builders' work. Each was a sculpture, a true piece of art.

In just a few short days they would roll their creations into the back of the trailers and close the door, hauling their dream to the next show, the next rally, the next big chance for their big break.

I envied them.

My phone vibrated on my hip and Leon's voice was in my ear before the second ring, nearly screaming over the din.

"Jaci? I've got a freaking parking lot over here! Pinstripe City has 'em backed up so far people can't get to my tent – they're walking right past me!"

I had suffocated the smoke on the painted cinder block wall and was already on my way across the lot.

"I'll be right there."

Beep

"Hello?"

I gulped the last of my coffee and dropped my mug in the backseat of my golfcart.

"Jaci? Yeah, this is Master Exhaust. I got empty boxes stacked up everywhere over here. My techs can't get around the lifts… I keep seeing those kids with the trash bins in their cart driving by, but they never stop!"

"I'll take care of it. They're probably jammed up because of traffic. I'll see if they can jump over there before they make the next round."

"You're the best, Jaxon."

2

"Awww, thanks, Les."

My heart smiled, but my face was too tired. It was chaotic. Demanding. Exhausting. And I loved it.

I had harbored hope over the last few years that this would be my life – albeit on a bigger scale - for a long time to come. The incessant ringing of my phone was, in my opinion, a nod of appreciation from the people who traveled across the country for another shot at making ends meet for their businesses, their staff, and their families. I had grown to know them personally, and love them genuinely. I felt they had connected to me. I was important to them, at least for this week, and it felt good. I was proud to wear my event shirt with the patch on the back marking me as "staff".

However, as the years wore on, I found myself struggling against the definition. I had always been proud of my answer to the introductory question; "So, what do you do?" but lately I wanted something more. I wanted to be this important for more than a couple of weeks at a time. I wanted to matter. All year.

For now, though, there was this – the Rally – and thoughts of my life, career, and future were quickly drowned out with phone calls, errands and management details. For now, for today, I was important to it. For now, I belonged here.

"I happen to know you haven't eaten all day, Jaci!" Selene hollered as I approached the collection of picnic tables marking the concessions area of the lot. I pulled my phone from my ear mid-sentence to check the time. *Damn. 2:30 already?* I grinned as I passed in front of the winding line of bikers at her tent. "Here." She thrust a plate of nachos out across the table and I shouldered my phone as I passed, scooping it up and nodding at her with gratitude.

"I'll have her there in 10 minutes, Raleigh. That's the best I can do in this traffic. You'll have to stall," I said as I dropped my nachos gently on the white leather seat of the cart.

"Fine." he said hurriedly and hung up.

A few seconds later I heard his best radio voice bellowing over the speakers on the front of the building.

"And we're back at Black Hills Harley-Davidson® for the Sturgis Motorcycle Rally, waiting for Miss MotorcycleTV. There are so many bikes packing this lot we had to send someone to pick her up from the interstate. So for now, we'll give you a little Guns 'n' Roses and we'll be back with our exclusive interview in ten minutes. This is 97.3 and we wanna know… are you ready to ROCK?!" A small cheer went up across the cluster of bikers milling about near the speakers.

I grinned.

After I delivered the Miss, I parked my cart between two semi trailers and took refuge in the back corner of one of my favorite vendors' tents.

"We've got to get you one of these riding vests, darling," Marian cooed as I stood in the shade behind the makeshift walls and shoveled chips dripping with something resembling cheese into my mouth. "This one is perfect for you. It would go great with that new bike I heard about." She held up a plain black leather vest, strung with black leather laces down the front.

I swallowed, then laughed.

"I don't know… it's just a little 500," I told her, trying not to hurt her feelings. "Honestly, it looks more like a rocket than a Harley. I'm not sure if leather is the way to go." I smiled. "How'd you find out anyway?"

"Oh honey, you know how we talk 'round here. Everybody is real happy for you. And proud too. Such a little lady on her own bike. You've got to get something for it… maybe a decal?"

I laughed again. "Thanks, Marian, but I am absolutely not little. Besides, you'd have to convince Jensen to give me a raise before I could afford that." I winked and nodded at the leather vest in her hand.

"And it's already got a little butterfly sticker on the fender. That's enough." I saw her face fall as she turned away to return the item to its rack, and I ached for her - for all of them. For most, every sale meant they were just a little bit closer to making money this year, that they could pay the bills for one more day. I'd have bought something from every last one, whether I needed it or not, if I had the resources to do so. I looked at her back and wiped at my face, making a mental note to stop by when it was all over and buy a patch or something. "Honestly, right now, all I really need is water," I told her.

Her face brightened and she stuck a finger in the air.

"Coming right up!"

I had just cracked the seal on the plastic bottle when Mason called.

"I didn't know I needed a fucking sales tax license! Where the fuck do I go to get that?"

I pulled the phone away to let him finish his rant at a more appropriate distance from my ear drum while I poured half the contents of the plastic bottle in my mouth, and when there was a degree of quiet on the other end, I replied; "It's in your book. Under the 'legal stuff' tab."

"Oh, shit. Would have been nice to know that."

"That's why I gave you a book, Mason." I made my words smile, as I looked out across the lot to see the sun drifting toward "late afternoon". I nodded at Marian, lifting my bottle in thanks and headed back toward the building. "You just need to fill out some on-line forms and that should take care of it. Let me know if you need anything else."

I heard him grunt a response but I couldn't make it out before he hung up.

My desk was barely showing under a pile of paper and binders, notes scribbled on legal pads and long lists of things to do that I hadn't been able to get to yesterday. I updated spreadsheets and sent them off to Jensen; the General Manager, and my boss. I sorted through my notes, checked my email, returned phone calls and re-organized my piles for tomorrow. It seemed only moments had passed when the digital clock in the corner of my screen blinked 7:00pm, marking the last hour of the day. I chugged down a huge container of water, descended the stairs and pushed through the glass doors of the building.

"How was it today?" I asked as I passed from one tent to another down the six long aisles of the parking lot. Responses were mixed and I took note of them, making mental records of what I could do next year to improve the experience. For most, nothing short of pulling the cash out of customers' wallets would have made a difference, but generally they were happy to be there, and they treated me as a friend.

Randy Tenevent of C-Force Clutches was standing at the corner of his tent with two visibly cold cans of beer and a smile as I rounded the corner of the last aisle.

"Only six more days," he said with a grin as he pulled the aluminum tab and thrust the can in my direction.
I nodded and smiled, gratefully taking a sip and a seat in the doorway of his trailer.

"Thanks. I've been waiting for this all day. How's the clutch business?" I asked, pouring the ice-cold fluid down my throat.

"Eh. Better than last year, I guess. Seems like traffic's up. How you holding up?"

"Eh. Better than last year, I guess," I said with a grin.

"Heard you got a bike. What is it?"

"Just a little Buell® Blast. It's perfect for me though; not too big, and I can put both feet down."

He laughed. "Yeah, that's probably good. You been riding much?"

"Oh yeah, I was riding every day before they started flooding in." I gestured to the lines of bikers pulling out of the parking lot headed for concerts, campgrounds, and bars.

"I just didn't want to ride in Rally traffic yet."

"Good choice, sweetheart. A lot of these riders come out here, aren't really ready for this level of riding. 'Specially with 400,000 other bikes on the road."

I sipped and nodded.

"You guys got world-class riding out here – some of those roads are pretty dangerous. 'Specially if you got some nut from Flat-and-Straight, USA thinking they can do the pigtails at 60." He shook his head.

"Or a brand-new rider on the road." I grinned.

He nodded with a wry smile.

"Didja take the safety course?"

"Yeah. I got in a little trouble though. They said I took the corners too fast." I shot him a guilty look. "But they passed me anyway."

He laughed out loud.

"Just remember, kid… always be just a little afraid of 'em." We both looked over the gleaming V-Rod perched on its kickstand in front of us.

"Yeah, I don't think that will be a problem," I said. "I still take it pretty easy. And I'm always just a tiny bit nervous. It's so light and small… I think I can manage it pretty well."

"I'm sure you can," he said. "It's the other guys I'm worried about."

I gave him a half-smile, my heart warming at his genuine concern. He drained the last of his can and dropped it in the trash.

"I don't think we can put our clutch on a Buell®, but…" he twisted around to retrieve something from inside the trailer. "How about a nice C-Force hat?"

I laughed and accepted his gift with gratitude.

"Hey, you guys aren't hiring, are you?"

"No," he said, drawing the response out with a curl in his grin. "You done with 20 hour shifts or what?"

"Ha. Ha." I said. "I only put in 12 - 14 and it's only for a couple weeks. But then some of these guys want to have a beer afterward…" I grinned at him. "You're eating up my nightlife."

He laughed. "You go out after this? You're crazy."

"God, no." I said as I emptied the can. "The first year I did, but I'm too old for that crap now."

He cracked another one and had it in my hand before I had flattened the first on the asphalt.

He scoffed. "What? You 22?"

"26." I wasn't, not quite yet, but my birthday was only days away and I didn't want to tell him that.

"I'm on the downhill slope to 30 Randy. Time to start slowing it down a bit."

He smiled and nodded in concession.

"Seriously? You're looking for another job?"

"Kind of."

"What, they not paying you enough?"

"No, no. It's not that... I love this job. The money is fine. And I like helping you guys out," I said, then took a long drink. "I don't even mind the hours. It's the other ten months that I'm ready to be done with. It can be boring, sometimes... I want... more." I filled my mouth with cold liquid again. It was delicious, and refreshing and I was grateful for it.

"Well, I'm sure you could get a job with any one of these vendors out here."

"You think? I've been secretly hoping for that. Honestly, I think I'd like to move again."

We both looked out at the thick ribbon of bikers on the interstate below us, headed for Sturgis under the reddening clouds.

"You don't like it here?"

"Oh, I do. It's beautiful. It's just... I don't know. I feel like I'm missing something, you know? I want *more*, Randy." I shook my open hands, delicately balancing the aluminum can between my fingers.

"So you want Jensen's job?"

I grinned broadly and swallowed.

"Maybe, yeah. But we both know that ain't happening. He isn't going anywhere. It's more than that, even. I keep thinking I'd be happier in a city... like I'd have a better chance to do something really great in a bigger place. I just don't feel like I'm *doing* anything. I feel like I'm just barely getting through it, you know?" I took another quick swig.

"Don't get me wrong, I love you guys," I said again, the words touched with a playful sarcasm and genuine sincerity. "I love my job... I'm just ready for... something."

"Like chase bikers all over the country in a trailer? It ain't as glamorous as you think, Jaxon. You know I haven't seen my wife in three months? It'll be another month or so before I get home and then I'll sleep for a week and hole myself up in my office for another." He shook his head and gulped the last of his second beer. "Three weeks after that I'm off to Daytona for Biketoberfest®."

I shrugged and cocked my head to one side. "I don't know what else to do, Randy. This is the job I have loved the most, but it's just not... I dunno... enough? Maybe if I was doing this for a bigger dealership, or a bigger rally..."

He scoffed. "Bigger than Sturgis? Sweetheart, nothin' 'cept the numbers will ever be bigger than Sturgis. This is the king of rallies."

"Oh, I know," I said, grinning. "I grew up listening to all the crazy stories of what it used to be like. Back when everybody camped in the city park and it was still about the races."

Randy laughed. I smiled.

"But a rally that's bigger in numbers means more planning, more organizing, more... everything." My voice sounded as though I were pleading with him. "I want this," I gestured around me in a semi-circle, "to last all year. It would, if I were doing this in Daytona." I paused and looked at him. "Or for a builder that travels to all of 'em."

He laughed and slapped my back. His short, knotted hands told the story of a hard life and belied his youth.

"Well, whatever you do, you'll be great at it kid."

"Thanks Randy. I hope so."

I was sure he saw the defeat in my eyes, but I did my best to hide it with a smile and rose my can to his.

"Happy rally," I said as I gulped the last of it and crushed the second can.

"You guys have a recycling bag around here?"

He laughed at me and shook his head.

"Hippie"

"Yup. And proud of it."

I grabbed the rest of his empties out of his trash and threw my arm up, crowning it with a peace sign as I walked away. "You guys have a good night. Drive safe."

"See you tomorrow." He hollered at my back.

My legs and feet were way past aching and pushing toward numb as dusk settled on the horizon and I trudged toward my car. The thunder of bikes had moved to the interstate now, vendors' tents zipped closed and a semblance of quiet descended on the lot. My heart softened. I would miss this.

***

The tiny apartment welcomed me with relative quiet and the smell of age I had grown to love over the years. I dropped onto the Lovesac® – a giant, very expensive pillow - with the fan working overtime and sipped whiskey. The PBS special was decidedly not that and I stared out the open window anticipating Trevor's return, my mind wandering over the day that had passed and the one that was yet to come.

I was exhausted, not just physically, emotionally. I could feel change coming. Something big. It had to. The restlessness had hit a fever pitch.

I pulled on my favorite pair of pajama pants and a too-big Tshirt, poured my drink into a coffee cup and headed downstairs.

The air was cool, soft, and too dry even for August. The concrete stair beneath me seemed to sap the heat from my body. I leaned against the door and let it melt away. Clusters of bikers passed me on the street in various stages of drunk, laughing and chatting and looking sideways at me. I ignored them and pulled out a cigarette.

A heavy, dark mass that had been forming in the pit of my stomach was mirrored in the most remote places of my heart. The time I had hoped would help it heal, only fed the ache. I was tired – tired of trying to find…. whatever it was I was looking for. I wasn't suicidal, I was exhausted. Done.

The feeling was that of having come upon the sudden end of a winding path. I was certain I had not taken a wrong turn, but here I was facing an emotional, diamond shaped yellow sign with thick block letters "DEAD END".

My phone rang for the last time that night and Trevor's name came up on the screen.

"Hey."

"Hi."

"What are you doing?"

"Outside smoking."

"Can I come over?"

My stomach tightened but I obliged, snapping the phone closed and suffocating the butt on the sidewalk. It wasn't that I didn't care about him. He was a wonderful man and I was grateful for him. We'd met at work. I'd been drawn to his quiet demeanor, his captivating eyes, and eventually I loved his heart. He was attentive, handsome, and quietly strong. He had made it possible for me to own my first motorcycle, even while still digging out from under old debts, and encouraged me to ride. His grace and power with his machine had inspired me and though I was afraid of it at first, to be sure, I was far more excited and I quickly fell in love with the bike and the ride. I felt independent and confident astride the little motor. I felt in control with the throttle in my hands and it was a nice feeling for a change.

He had been a tremendous blessing in my life, but we weren't really right for each other and I had been ignoring that truth for months.

I was almost asleep on the Lovesac® when he finally came through the door, dropping his jacket and pulling off his bandana with a chunk of hair still tied in the knot.

"How was it today?" I asked absently, watching scenes from the streets of New York flicker by on the screen before me.

"Brutal." He said as he poured thick, honey colored liquid over three cubes of ice. "My line was never less than 25. All freaking day. Everybody wants those new spark plugs and they're backordered for a month. Pisses people off."

He sipped, and curled his lips under as he swallowed. "Vane was so slow people kept jumping over... Walter did better though."

I nodded and looked back at the TV.

"I saw you go by a couple times today. No time to meet your boyfriend for lunch, huh?"

He was teasing but my heart flamed.

"It was a little hectic today," I said and took another swig.

He dropped in next to me and even as I felt his arm around my shoulders, I wanted to escape. Instead I managed a thin smile.

"I'm gonna go smoke."

"I thought you just did."

"Yeah... an hour ago. It's just the day, I guess... and the whiskey."

The ice clinked in my coffee cup and my pajama pants dragged the floor with each step down the dark, narrow hallway, blue carpet stained brown in the center from years of wear. My earlier station was vacant again and I sat, my arms on my knees, and let most of the cigarette burn away. The dark and cool were soothing, the city would soon be sleepy. I closed my eyes and took a deep breath.

Four years here. I hadn't meant to stay. I was just going to get my feet back under me again. I had finally come fully out of the hole I had dug for myself and for that I was grateful, and proud. The road ahead, however, looked like more of the same and I didn't like it. The yearning in my heart made it ache and I looked down at the stoop beneath me as I blew out the last drag. Same dark stains from what I guessed to be a combination of ancient gum and road grime. The same crack on the lowest stair edge. The same teetering plastic lamp post.

The Me I Was

I'd been here before. Pretty much every day for the last four years. *Who am I kidding? I've been here since I was 13.* Always searching. Always unsettled, always looking for something.

I pushed the thought out of my mind and sent out a silent hope one of the custom shops would ask me to join their adventure and take to the road.

Standing, I dropped the butt in the sidewalk trash can and swung my hip hard into the door of the building, mounting the stairs as the heavy thing swung shut behind me.

Trevor was watching the Comedy Channel when I dropped my lighter on the table by the door. "Drake wants us to meet for dinner at Rosa's Saturday night. His wife is in town this week. I have Saturday off… think you can cut out early?"

I filled a jar with water as he spoke, gulped down half, and emptied the rest on the drooping peace lily.

"Sounds like fun. I'll have to check with Jensen, but I think he'll be OK with it."

He flipped channels as sleep began to overtake me and an hour later he roused me to move to bed.

***

"You been drinking enough water?" Jensen asked as he passed me in the coffee line.

I grinned and nodded.

"Don't want to send you back to the hospital this year."

The memory made me blush. The heat and exhaustion and too little water had landed me in the Emergency Room with heat stroke the year before.

We both laughed and he pushed his knuckled fist into mine.

"Happy Birthday," he smiled.

I had rather forgotten I'd crossed into the high-side of 'mid-twenties' today and when the smiling barista took my order she handed it back to me with a wink.

"On the house today. Happy Birthday!"

I raised my cup in thanks and pulled my phone from its belt clip. First call of the day.

A tricked out golf cart cruised past me, then pulled hard back to the left, lifting the front tire slightly off the ground and swinging sideways to park in front of me. Gus pulled a cigarette from his pack and held it up with raised eyebrows. I shook my head and smiled, taking a seat next to him. "…Uh huh. I'll have them to you in a half hour." I nodded at Gus. "Bye." I snapped my phone closed and he navigated us at a much more appropriate speed to a quiet corner near the front entrance of the lot.

"About a hundred and fifty parked at the gate already. It's gonna be big today. 'Course last couple days always are," he said as he lit a smoke and passed it to me.

I nodded and sipped from the black plastic lid. "Should be a good one for the vendors then."

"How you doin' this year?" he asked as he tapped the end of his pack against his palm, pulling out a second smoke for himself.

I shrugged.

"Better than last year. I'm way more organized. My phone rings half as often."

His turn to nod. "Good."

We sat in silence, watching tents unzip across the lot. The heat rising from the asphalt was already giving an eerie fluid look to the horizon.

"Whatcha doin' for your birthday?"

I shrugged. "I dunno. Probably nothing, honestly. I'm getting too old to party anymore."

He laughed. "I heard Eric's old lady 'bout left him for good after your party last year."

I shot him a look of feigned astonishment. "That was not my fault." I insisted and took a drag. "First of all, Trevor took me out there so we'd have a chance for a little bit of quiet. I don't think he even knew the builder boys would be there. Secondly, Seth had been drawing on the table with a magic marker, and wanted to give me a birthday tat… so he drew

14

some crazy design on my back. Eric was just holding up the back of my shirt to look at it… The other hand just happened to be on my hip when she came around the corner."

Gus was laughing so hard his eyes were watering.

"Yeah, I guess it probably looked pretty bad." I giggled.

Gus wiped his eyes.

"There was definitely too much tequila." I conceded. "Still, one of my best birthdays to date."

"Tequila girl, huh?"

"Yea, but not too much. I'm OK with a little buzz once in awhile, but I don't like to be drunk. I like to remember."

"Well, maybe we can have a little nip before you take off for the day. Gotta do something… it's your birthday."

I gave him a broad smile, took my last drag and squeezed the cherry onto the blacktop. "Hey - will you stop by American Leather? They complained about their power going out after the rain last night." Gus nodded.

"I better run. Sonic Sound needs some copies made before we open up."

"All right, kid. I'll see if I can catch you for lunch."

My legs were already sore when I stepped out of the cart and headed east across the asphalt. *Two more days.*

***

Gus found me at Sin City Customs enjoying a beer as the boys pushed one gorgeous bike after another into the trailer for the night. When he pulled a traveler of Jose Cuervo out of his jacket I laughed out loud.

He grinned and took a swig before handing me the bottle.

"You're a trip, Gus" I said and took a little pull, chasing the burn with the last of my Miller Lite.

"How was the birthday?" he asked.

"Good. Uneventful. I think I finally kinda know how to take care of these guys."

The boys in the back laughed.

"Eh. There's a few things you still won't do," one shot out to us.

We all laughed. I blushed.

I was fully aware that I wasn't getting this kind of attention because I was special, or particularly beautiful. Especially when these guys watched super model bodies walk by all week long clad in little more than patches of leather lashed to their bodies with sinew. Especially when I was 'stocky' at best with skin peppered by pimples. I was just friendly, and here. I knew it. Still, it felt nice, so I let it flutter in my stomach and flush my face.

It was easy to feel good here.

I enjoyed a second beer over fits of laughter and conversation as the sun sunk behind the hills, and then headed for home.

***

Saturday dawned and I dragged myself around the lot, helping vendors get the last of their business handled before they packed up. I was tired and it was as much in my heart as in my body. Fourteen days and no new job, no big change, nothing. One by one they closed up their trailers, tore down their tents and pulled out, and with them my hopes for… change.

The six o'clock sun was still high in the summer sky when I dropped my clipboard on my desk and switched off the lights. The heaviness in my bones was more powerful than ever before and the smiles I shared with the exhausted staff as I passed them were hallow and forced.

My mood had improved some by the time I emerged from the shower. Dinner at Rosa's sounded good – a quaint Mom and Pop well known for it's incredible steak and decadent desert menu - and I was looking forward to the ride. I twisted my still-wet hair into a braid, dressed in my best jeans, and got back into my car.

I shoved the gearshift into park in front of Trevor's house, and sat for a moment listening to the quiet hum and staccato click of the motor cooling down while I finished my smoke. I was sure he knew something was wrong. I hoped he wrote it off as stress and exhaustion. It was, in part.

It wasn't him… I was the problem. I really was, and I knew it. I couldn't hold still. I couldn't settle down. I couldn't find what I was looking for… I couldn't even define it. I couldn't imagine living this life very long, so I certainly couldn't give him my future – not even a part in it, and I couldn't give him my heart.

I should have been happy. I had a great little apartment, a job I liked that was – at least for the summer – fast paced and interesting, a boss I enjoyed, a man I cared about, a paycheck that covered the bills… but there was no "happy". Something had to change, something big. It wouldn't be fair - to either of us - to continue pretending I believed in a future together. Hell, I couldn't even believe in a future for me. I had hoped a new career would take care of the problem for me, but it hadn't. Now, not only did I *not* have a great new job, but I had to find a way to tell Trevor that I wasn't happy and needed to be alone. I couldn't imagine what I would say that could get me out without hurting him, but my smoke was out, and sitting here staring out the window wasn't helping. I pushed the ashtray closed and pulled my bag out of the passenger seat.

The black beauty was parked just outside the garage near the back of the driveway, its freshly polished chrome shining in the sun as I moved past it heading for the house. The sight of it made me smile. I loved that bike. He'd even let me drive it once, when I'd first finished the safety course, but my legs were too short to touch and he'd had to hold it up from the seat behind me until I could get the kickstand down. I'd been embarrassed, but he'd been kind - and quiet. A few months later he'd loaned me the money to buy the Buell and I couldn't have been more grateful.

Trevor was an exceptional rider. We were good together, too – at least on the bike. His slight frame and short stature belied the mass of the Harley-Davidson® that sat easily beneath him. He maneuvered it as though it were an extension of him, a sensual, mechanical beast he could guide through graceful curves and spur to its limit down long stretches of highway. Arms wrapped around him, I could feel the dance, I could surrender to his aptitude and swoon to the beat of the heaving cylinders, release my weight to the strength and grace, and be gone. I loved it.

He was with his parents on the patio, sipping tea and idly chatting when I rounded the corner.

"Jaci!" His mother said. "You look great!"

I grinned and blushed.

"Everybody looks great after their first real post-rally shower," I said.

We all laughed.

Trevor looked good too, in a new Tshirt and jeans, his tan rivaling mine, the color of his skin almost as dark as his eyes. He stood up and hugged me, and I could feel the tenderness of his heart in his touch. I had just finished tying on my bandana when his Mom leapt to her feet.

"Wait! I want a picture," she said, hustling into the house and returned camera in hand.

"You both just look so nice," she said grinning almost apologetically. My heart softened at her sentiment. I loved her... his father, and his sister... I loved him. I loved them. Genuinely. It would be hard, when the time came, but it was not now.

He wrapped his arm around me and I tucked myself into his embrace, turning sideways to give the camera a tired smile. It was a celebration to be sure. It always was when we got done with rally. Months of planning and weeks of long hours and monumental effort were over and in a week or so we'd get fat paychecks and days off. The joy was there, we were all just too tired to show it.

I pulled on my jacket and dropped my sunglasses onto the bridge of my nose.

"Whaddya think? Should we wear 'em?" he asked when we had moved around the corner to the bike, shoving his arm through the opening in his leather jacket.

I screwed up my face and looked at him in confusion.

"Wear what?"

"The helmets. Do you think we should wear them?"

I screwed up my face again.

"No. Why?"

We'd been riding together the better part of two years and had only worn them once – on his sport bike – and that was only because we were *planning* to go well over 100 mph. They were big, hot, and awkward. Mine was always smacking the back of his, I couldn't see well and it made holding onto him impossibly uncomfortable. Right or wrong, we'd never done it and I couldn't understand why he would want to do so now.

He shrugged and got on. I followed suit, taking part in a graceful routine we had perfected over the years swinging my leg over the saddle of the iron horse, seating my body squarely behind him, and leveraging my legs into the gap between the pegs and shocks. The sound of the motor was familiar, soothing, and I let out a quiet sigh of relief, wrapping one arm across his sculpted belly as he eased the bike between his parent's cars and out of the driveway. They were standing shoulder to shoulder, smiling, in the very place we'd been, his father's arm around his mother's waist when I looked back to wave goodbye.

The Harley-Davidson® Dyna eagerly scaled the steep highway into the Hills, through the first corners and as the trees lining the road blurred to a grey-green wash, I let the stress of the week and the diamond shaped yellow sign drift out of my mind. I could smell the intensity of the season, the earth dry and sapped of its moisture. It was still fully hot at 7pm, even with the wind whipping past at 75 miles per hour.

The dance had begun. I rested my chin on his shoulder and watched the road before us as if the throttle were in my hands. He tested the physics of balance, rode the very edge with delicate precision and complete control - and I loved it. Especially with him.

I had learned his pattern, and he, mine. I knew where he instigated the turn, pressing the bike onto it's rubber edge, where he crested the corner and then let the powerful forward motion pull us gently back to upright, all the while holding a perfect line mimicked in paint on either side of the tires. Occasionally I encouraged an even more aggressive turn, gently shifting my weight just a little more into the curve of the corner.

I connected with it, with him, and basked in the world around me; the sights and smells. I felt certain of myself there with the thunder of the motor beneath me. I felt the way I always wanted to feel; quietly powerful, calm, balanced, unexpectedly graceful, and just a little bit wild.

I firmed my grip against him as we sailed into a tight and familiar corner and we held our line hugging the narrow shoulder. Sparks shot off the foot pegs as they often did, skimming the surface of the road, laying a deep gouge in the asphalt. I sucked in a breath and then immediately let the feeling split my face in a broad grin. I was not afraid. I was free.

TWO
1999

The puppy had learned quickly, and pride turned to frustration as the little creature nosed the jingle bell dangling from the door knob every few minutes, then thumped her tail on the floor as she sat and waited to go outside.

"Jeshanti! We just came in. Come over here and play with your toy."

The little wiggling mass nosed the bell again.

Sighing, I turned up the television.

Summer passed outside the tall windows of my first apartment as I lazed away the days watching Breakfast at Tiffany's and smoking too many cigarettes.

A modest job at a local bank had given me the resources to stay in my now-sleepy college community and live on my own for the first time. Three stories up in one of the oldest buildings in town, my "home" was a cramped studio that stunk of age and mildew, but I loved it. I loved what it represented. I was an adult. Self-sufficient and in complete control of my future - mostly, anyway.

I could buy whatever I wanted – as long as the modest salary I made at First National covered it. I could have a dog – three if I wanted, and a flop-eared rabbit to boot. And I did. I could stay out with friends until 4 in the morning and drive to the city on the weekends. But that, I didn't do.

I stayed home, with the dogs and the rabbit and hid in my room. I didn't really have any friends, and I didn't have the courage to go out alone. I smoked more of my grocery money than I would admit and watched the only movie I had; Breakfast at Tiffany's.

Freshman year at State had not been the magic experience of my dreams. My high school boyfriend Charlie had graduated two years earlier, and had waited for me so we could go to college together. His age had made him eligible for off-campus housing, and so his apartment was where we spent almost all our time. I made no new friends, went to no parties, saw almost none of the town.

When Charlie went home for the summer I found an apartment and told him it was time to go our separate ways. I kept my part-time bank job and spent all the money I made on rent, and cigarettes and dog food. It was as though the freedom had been too much. I had no idea what to do with it – with myself in it. The sheer weight of endless possibility glued me to my grandparent's old couch in my tiny living room and there I stayed, next to the only window, blowing smoke through the screen, pining after Holly Golightly's bohemian, free spirited life. She was confident, and widely loved, almost because of her fierce independence and staunch "I do what I want and I take care of myself" attitude. She was brave, and playful, and I was utterly smitten with living that kind of life.

As Audrey Hepburn stood facing the windows of the towering jewelry store for the third time this day, I dreamed of myself in an elegant black dress, eating whatever tickled my tongue at the moment and living from one party to the next. It seemed the city itself was the key. Bursting with endless possibility and constant change, you couldn't help but bump into a life of magic. You could be whoever you wanted to be. There was a place for everyone in New York. I had been once, long ago, and the memory was flushed with fondness. New York felt... special.

A moment later I turned off the TV and snatched my keys from the counter. "Peanuts! Stephanie! Let's go!" Peanuts - the toy poodle - squeezed through the door at the same time as Stephanie - the standard - by trotting through under her belly. I laughed at the tangle of them tumbling down the stairs. I locked the door and, carrying Whiskers the lop-eared angora decked out in his harness, trotted down after them. "Come on Jeshanti." The little Rottweiler puppy was close on my heels and quickly piled into the car with the others.

We stopped at the park for a break and after tying Whiskers' leash to a tree, I stretched out in the grass next to him. His nose was going a hundred miles an hour and I imagined him savoring the taste of the fresh grass he munched on. The dogs ran and chased, sniffed and barked, and after a sufficient romp, all three lay in the grass panting. I untied Whiskers lead, and followed him around as he stretched his legs and took in the smells.

New York. New York?! I shook my head at the thought. There was no way. Even without the poodles - I was just watching them for the summer while my parents built their new house - there was no way I would be able to afford a place to live. Especially on the salary of a teenage loan assistant. Defeat flickered in my mind for only a moment. New York was too big, too much, too far.

Denver however, was not. I grinned at the idea. Denver, I could pull off. Denver was big, too... full of opportunity. I could be a mountain woman, me and my rabbit, and my dog - and that sounded nice. My little zoo followed me back to the car, and there they waited while I scrolled through the Denver Post Classifieds on a computer the size of a milk crate at the University library.

"Wanted: Executive Assistant. Responsibilities include answering phones, filing and general office duties. Call 307-555-5555."

I called two other ads and two days later my pups were my passengers as I headed for interviews in the closest big city.

I stayed with my parents the first night, and left all the animals in their care for the day. I could drive down and back if I left at 4am, and I'd be home for a late dinner. Rest was fitful, and I had already had a full cup of coffee by the time dawn touched the horizon.

I cried as I passed through the wide open plains, the mountains and the sun rising before me, a delicate shade of blue against a pink sky. *What the hell am I doing?* This would be my home now – my new life. This place I hardly knew, a place where I had no friends, no money, no real plan… This was what I wanted. Wasn't it? A place where no one knew me, where I could be whomever I wanted to be. A place where I could find the kind of life I wanted. A place where I could find the part of the world where I belonged. When my chest settled to a normal rhythm, I made myself smile. *Well, why the hell not?* It sure beat going back to my tiny apartment and watching the same old movie over and over every day.

The summer sun was well above the mountains when I pulled into a gas station set katty-corner from the road where I was to launch this new life with a good job… I hoped. I entered the single stall restroom in my gym pants and a tshirt, and was grateful to find it unoccupied, large, and with a locking door. It did not take me long to change and twist my hair up into a bun and I emerged in my best all-business skirt and blazer, wearing heels and toting an empty briefcase. I resumed my journey and a short while later stood in the doorway of the offices of Independent Investors Inc.

The look in his eyes when the chestnut door swung open told me he was impressed. So was I. Tall, with hair a lazy shade of brown and eyes the color of kiwi, he was handsome. The office was simple, but very professional. His desk was large, rich mahogany, and the framed certificates and awards on the walls behind him boasted quietly of his success. From behind his desk he smiled as we spoke, but not so often as to appear more than polite. I liked him.

The feeling was mutual, apparently, as I passed the last exit out of the city suburbs toward home and answered his call on my cell phone. The job was mine. I had to start the day after tomorrow or not at all. I made arrangements to stay with the parents of an old friend and called my bank job from the car as I turned around, headed for my new life.

The Me I Was

My sister Jess had already fallen in love with Whiskers and agreed to take charge of the zoo until I could find a place of my own. My friend's family was accommodating and patient while I camped in their spare bedroom. It was an hour drive each way to my new job, but I enjoyed it. A cup of coffee, a wide selection of radio music and an hour on the road was a great way to start my day... and wind down at the end. After I got my first full paycheck I moved into a brand new apartment with a suitcase, a bar of soap and bottle of shampoo, and a pair of bowls for Jeshanti's dinner.

The new job was more interesting than I thought it would be and my new boss had big plans for me, a blueprint for my life he laid out on a napkin over lunch one afternoon approaching September.

He had grown up in New York, he said, as our salads were delivered to our table. He had dropped out of high school and came west with a cousin. They slept in a van, ate when they had the money, and schemed their days and nights away with plans to make their fortune. Eventually Peter started Independent Investors Inc., a company built on venture capitalists, and had made his first million before he was 35.

As our plates were cleared he pulled a pen from his suit pocket and smoothed the napkin delivered with his beer. He drew the profile of a face, pointed out the different areas of the brain and talked about how his kind of success could be achieved by living in certain areas of the mind.

"I want you to basically do what Resse has done," he said, after our plates were cleared. "I'll take you to meet her tomorrow. She works in our southern Colorado office. Started with me 5 years ago, about your same age. She's running the branch down there now, my right-hand woman. Making a lot of money too. Has a nice house, cabin in Durango. I'm sending her to start another branch up there next month..."

He looked at me. I smiled. I nodded. My stomach got tight and my mind was spinning. I wasn't sure if the message I was getting was the right one.

I didn't wonder long. He leaned back in his chair, looked at me again, then leaned forward to spell it out for me. I'd work as the office manager here in Denver for a few years, then start my own branch. I'd be running a few branches, making six figures before I was 30, and how did that sound?

I swallowed hard, and smiled. It sounded great, I told him, and smiled again.

***

The "big city" apartment was actually just outside of the city itself, situated in an everything's-the-same kind of middle class neighborhood in a just-like-the-others suburb. The apartment complex was so new they were still putting in the grass, rolling it out one strip at a time as I clicked past on the sidewalk leading up to my new front door. The apartment smelled like paint and carpet glue. It was huge - compared to my first, and populated entirely by my suitcase, and my puppy.

I gave her a scratch, set my keys on the counter with Peter's napkin, and pulled a smoke from my pack. Jeshanti wandered around in the new grass sniffing out the perfect place to pee while I smoked, watching the day fade away. Venture Capitalist, huh? I had to admit the security of an income that big did sound nice. It was a good opportunity, at the very least. It would certainly fast-track the success of my adult life.

Back inside I fed my pup and plopped down in my favorite spot in the center of the living room where the light from outside came through the big window and framed me on the floor. With a fork and can opener in one hand and a can of green beans in the other I set about "making" dinner. I never much liked green beans. Even when they were straight from the garden. But these had been on sale so I'd stocked up.

The Me I Was

I'd found a book in the trunk of my car the first weekend in my new place, one that I had read ages ago, and buried myself in its pages while I ate. When I put it down to go to the bathroom I stared at the blank walls, at the wide expanse of carpet in the huge, empty bedroom. I had thought Denver would be the key. I thought it would be the place where I would be swept up in the culture - the art, the music, the outdoorsy lifestyle - and discover that I was that kind of person. I thought I'd spend Thursday nights enjoying a glass of wine with friends at the jazz lounge or at parties downtown, and weekends backpacking or attending art festivals in the little mountain towns. But I didn't. I wasn't.

I wasn't Holly Golightly, spending my days window shopping. I was hiding, losing myself in my job, or my book, or my bed. There was no money for lounges or shopping. Or parties. Or traveling. Not yet. But there could be... My stomach twisted a little when I thought about my conversation with Peter and I pushed the thought out of my mind. I was discouraged and lonely.

Dusk touched the clouds outside the single living room window with a delicate pink finger. I finished my canned green beans and washed my fork. It was far too early for bed, so I laid belly down on the floor and resumed my book. Jeshanti had no interest in that, of course, and in a desperate plea for attention, climbed on my back, took my ponytail in her mouth and threw her weight to her rear, pulling with all she was worth. I shrieked and rolled over to reprimand her, but her deep brown eyes were apologetic and playful. I softened. "Oh, all right. I know." I told her. She deserved play. I wrenched myself from the floor, clipped on her makeshift leash and we were out the front door.

The evening was beautiful, warm and still light enough, but I could not love it. More than a month here, and I had never loved it. Not like I wanted to, not like I thought I should. Passing through the park, my mind wandered. Even with Peter's long-term plan laid out for me, I could not see happiness here. I could only see a corner office stuffed with stress and a too-tight business suit. The money would be great, yes, but I wanted joy. My heart sank. *Maybe I shouldn't have quit school and moved,* I thought.

I desperately wanted my book and realized, as I dragged my pup toward home, nothing had changed. I still ignored the passing days. I was still smoking what little money I had. I was still looking for more. I had traded Breakfast at Tiffany's for Murder Mystery, but everything else was the same.

I was tired. I was tired of looking for happiness, tired of just getting by, just existing. I wanted to love life or be over with it already. It was not a happy life, for either of us.

I shouldn't have gotten the dog. I thought. She was looking at me with her eyes up and head down, discouraged, in front of our door. I felt the weight of guilt heavy on my heart. There was still wild in her, and puppy too. She needed to run willy-nilly through fields of long, waving grass and flop down in the sunshine heaving with the exertion and sheer joy of it. *Shit, I want that.* I couldn't give it to her, especially not here.

I smoked my last cigarette of the night and threw a ball for her in the courtyard, and as soon as I had again buried myself in the life of a big city medical examiner, she was on my back and tugging on my hair.

***

"I'm taking a road trip out to see Joe," he said.
His voice was comforting, even over the phone.

We'd started dating when I was a sophomore in high school and he, a senior. He had waited for me to graduate, and moved with me 300 miles to attend our Freshman Year at State. He had gone home for the summer when I bought the puppy and rented the smelly third story studio apartment. I had decided it was best for us to end our relationship and though he was not happy about it, we attempted to remain friends. It had only been a couple of months since he left me and my little zoo, but it felt like forever.

"In Washington? Nice! When are you going?"

"Three weeks. I gotta finish up a job over on the South Side and then I'm out of here for the rest of the fall. I'll be passing through Denver that first night. Can I stay with you?"

"Sure," I said, my heart fluttering in my chest.

Charlie had been my first real, serious boyfriend and though we were still in high school, he was my first, real love. His brassy voice brought back old memories and warmed my heart.

Life had been so easy when Charlie was around. He was smart and capable, cherished his family and worked hard. His job with a construction company had quickly turned him from a lanky High School boy covered in freckles into a man, with a body chiseled by labor and tanned by the sun. Charlie was beautiful, intelligent, and adored me. We'd naively planned to be married someday, long before our first semester at State, and I knew Charlie would have taken great care of me if I'd have let him. His voice in my ear brought back all those old feelings of security, respect, and love.

Now I sat on a bench outside my empty apartment, phone pressed to my ear, wallowing in the memory as he talked and smoking, the city humming and twinkling around me and the puppy tugging on her leash. I thought of Peter, and our visit with Reese just a few days before. She was a stunning woman, smart, and while I had admired her right away, she hadn't seemed exceptionally happy either.

"How's Jeshanti?" Charlie asked, pulling me back to the moment.

"Good. She's good." I paused. "I just don't really know what to do with her. I walk her every night but she's still got so much energy. She's tearing up the carpet in my new place and I can't afford a kennel or anything just yet.... I got her a rawhide, but she ate the whole thing in one night."

He laughed and I missed him.

"How long do you think you'll be gone?"

"Don't know. Until I run out of money, I guess."

"Can I come along?"

The question caught us both off guard. I had not planned to say such a thing. I hadn't even thought about it. It was wildly out of character and I would have considered it incredibly rude if someone had said it to me. I'm sure I would not have said it at all if it hadn't been Charlie.

I apologized, embarrassed, but he hesitated only a moment.

"Sure. Of course you can."

I flushed with excitement and hope.

The next day I gave my new job notice, packed my suitcase again, and three weeks later, left my bleeding heart with the puppy at the rescue shelter.

THREE

The sun was hot through the windshield as Diane headed into town for her evening ritual – a tall fast-food cup of Diet Coke.

After a long day, the bubbly elixir was more soothing even than the drive, a winding mountain road hugging the edge of sheer cliffs that sunk her gradually out of the hills away from her home and business, and the stress of the day.

The constant drone of motorcycles had waned over the last two days and she passed only a few stragglers, their belongings lashed to sissy bars and stuffed saddlebags as they headed out of town. The grasses bathing the swells on either side of the road were already surrendering their green to shades of yellow, orange and purple. The air was heavy and still. Tiny wisps on the edges of dense white clouds gathered on the horizon.

She sighed. It had been a long day. A long week. A long summer. Finally though, she was pushing through the last of her busy season and a well earned late fall vacation was quickly approaching. Her mind wandered as she navigated the turns, thoughts meandering through the coming week and a long to-do list.

Just inside the third big corner, across from Falling Rock, she frowned and instinctively pressed the brake. A small car was parked in the short grass to her right and a large truck in front of it had not quite pulled his bobcat-laden trailer fully out of the lane. The driver seemed confused as he paced near an open cab door with a phone pressed to his ear. She eased her SUV to the scant shoulder behind the compact and surveyed the scene.

Another young man with long hair tied back from his face with a brown bandana lay on the center line, dazed and disoriented. A handful of people were gathered around him, some on phones, others squatted next to him listening intently and talking quickly to each other. There was worry in the eyes of the gazes that met hers. Diane stepped out of her car and onto the pavement, and was headed toward the group when she realized her shoes were sticking to the asphalt. Her heart sank when she looked down. Blood. Everywhere. Spattered on the side of the bobcat and trailer, smeared in streaks across the doors of the truck and in the pattern of tire tread across the road. She hurried to join the tiny crowd gathered around the young man.

"Where's my girlfriend? I'm fine. Find my girlfriend," he muttered, rolling in and out of consciousness.

"There was someone else?" bystanders asked each other, each shrugging in response, having come upon the scene too late to have known anything about the parties involved. Each stunned face scanned the foot of the small cliff behind the cars, the grassy edge of the road and the gravel road leading back to hiking trails. All was clear.
Suddenly, adrenaline set Diane's feet alight when she spotted a still, crumpled body in the tall grasses of the embankment on the other side of the road. She took the slope quickly and with ease, calling out to a long haired woman blinking slowly.

She was young and her blonde braid lay stark against deeply tanned skin. Ignoring the mess of blood, she knelt at her side as the woman struggled to sit up. Diane worked herself into position behind her, letting the head of corn-silk hair lie back in her lap.

The woman was smiling but her deep green eyes were far away. Diane smoothed her hair and scanned her limp form for injuries. A sharp edge of white bone jutted out of the woman's jeans above her left knee, and the rest of the fabric hung in tatters, tangled with chunks of flesh from the knee down on both sides, exposing the muscle and bone. She could see the glistening white of tendons and the bright red of spasming muscle. A stream of blood pumping through an artery in her right thigh was running down what was left of her leg, pooling to form a puddle in the grass beneath them. Her breath was ragged and labored. This woman was going to die.

Diane blinked, stunned by the realization. Stroking the young woman's hair, she lifted her gaze to the sheer rock wall across from her. Sirens were growing louder in the background, flashing lights casting bright colors on the wall, and people hustled about. Someone was screaming that the helicopter couldn't land here, and that an ambulance from just up the road was on its way. It all seemed so surreal, so far away. She closed her eyes for a moment to take a breath and when she opened them again, the scene before her changed. The lights and gravel and asphalt turned to a vast green meadow, sunlight the color of gold bathing the vision in a soothing warmth. Moments stretched long, like pulled taffy, perfect calm descended upon them as the light grew and with it a sense of immense power. Looking out across the green meadow before her, Diane began to pray. "Our father, who art in heaven…"

An overwhelming sense of love bubbled in her, and the power of the light seemed to grow, bathing them both in peace. Warm, and calm, and infinite it flooded over and around them, seeping deep into Diane's spirit filling her with joy.

"WHAT HAPPENED?!" the voice came to her as though through a fog. Blinking, she looked up at the stranger running up the hill toward them. "I don't know," she said slowly, still stroking the flaxen hair and somewhat irritated by the interruption.

"Keep her awake! Take off her rings. Talk to her!" he instructed curtly as he fell to his knees and tore his shirt from his back. "What's two times two?" Diane addressed the face in her lap, still warm from her vision. "Questions she can answer!" the stranger chastised, looking first at Diane, and then into the young woman's face.

"My name is Alan and I am going to do everything I can to help you," he said shredding his shirt into strips. The young lady struggled to prop herself up awkwardly on a badly broken left arm and stuck out her right hand.

"I'm Jaci," she told him cheerfully. "Nice to meet you." She smiled, showing teeth stained with blood. He gave her a look of desperation, and with her looked down at his hands, furiously tying strips of a cotton polyester blend around her right thigh, above the spewing artery. Blinking slowly, she looked up at him again. "I don't feel very well," she announced and promptly lost consciousness.

FOUR
1999

The plan was to travel until we got low on money. We'd find jobs wherever we were and see where life took us. For the first time in years, I was not just excited, I was hopeful. Even the ache at the sight of the puppy's eyes when I left the shelter the night before could not sway my mind. Maybe everything I was looking for had been there with Charlie all along.

His smell was familiar, his embrace warm when he arrived on my new doorstep. I hadn't realized how much I had missed him until he was in front of me again - older, somehow, and shy. He immediately lit a cigarette and introduced me to the new love of his life; a 10 year old sports car, rare for it's brand, that showed little wear save for the dulled red paint. I nodded and smiled, ooh-ing and ahh-ing at what I assumed were the most unique features. I knew almost nothing about cars, but I could see his pride, and that alone was worth the attention.

Dinner at the Applebees in the nearest shopping plaza sounded delicious, as far as I was concerned, and by the time we had ordered our drinks, it was as if nothing had changed. He was so kind and attentive, such a gentleman. And he made me feel as though I were the most beautiful and important woman in the world. I felt safe with Charlie around. I could relax. I could enjoy. And I did.

Charlie and I sat in the courtyard of my building after dinner, enjoying a smoke and talking. Mine mostly burned away between my fingers as I told him about all that had been my life since I'd left him after school got out last spring. He laughed while I told my tales and my heart swelled at the sound.

I sat back on the bench when he joined me there, pulled on the cigarette and looked out into the twinkle of streetlights coming on. I exhaled and looked over at him, his gaze and mouth about to speak when suddenly he surrendered whatever it was he was going to say, took my face in his hands for a moment and kissed me.

Instantly I remembered it all. I knew his touch, his mouth, his smell. I knew how delicate I would feel when he pulled me closer, how strong his body would feel holding me against him. I knew how wildly romantic the whole thing would be in my memory when I dropped my cigarette and threw my arms around him. I knew better, so did he, but the sparks that rained between us would not be put out.

The next morning we crammed all our luggage around the huge speaker box in the back of the sportscar, had a hearty breakfast at Perkins and left for the coast. I was giddy with excitement. I had never felt like such a rebel, I'd never felt so free. The drive was beautiful - early fall touching the trees whipping by outside my window. We talked most of the first day, trading stories and laughter, and I remembered our first trip together, to the South Dakota State University in Brookings, South Dakota, almost exactly a year ago.

The summer after my senior year of High School was particularly warm and it had been a blistering August day. He'd worked 10 hours in the sun and was exhausted, but happy, when he picked me up from my parents house at 5 o'clock. I, however, was ecstatic This would be my first real road trip without them, my first trip with Charlie, and while we both knew I'd have to stay in the dorms for the orientation weekend, we also knew this experience marked the first days of our adult lives together. It felt like a switch had flipped and the light of "adulthood" was finally shining on me, growing brighter with every mile.

We'd spent the trip talking about God and our families, and dreaming about our futures as we chased a huge, beautiful lightening storm across the prairie. I'd been so impassioned by our conversation that I'd turned around in the passenger's seat, my back on the dashboard so we could see each other's faces while we talked. The energy between us was electric, sparked by our chatter and too many bottles of iced coffee and soda. It must have been around midnight when Charlie noticed the green South Dakota mile markers had turned blue. We'd gone too far and had crossed into Minnesota.

It seemed ages ago, now, staring out the window into the tree-lined interstate through the western half of Montana. So much in my life had changed, and yet so little had really changed at all. The crisp fall morning gave way to a bright afternoon as we passed Coeur d' Alene in Idaho. The lake shimmered in the sun outside my window and as Charlie negotiated traffic I let myself idly dream of life in a lake house. Mornings would be spent with coffee and the news on the deck over the lake, the sound of the surf lapping against the posts. On hot days I'd swim or walk the perimeter with my dog... The thought of the beautiful puppy I had just left behind broke my heart again and I pushed the image out of my mind before guilt could have her way with me and stared at the road ahead. Dusk was falling as I-90 climbed sharply through Washington and into the Cascades and just as traffic seemed to thin out the tiniest bit, a terrible rattle began under the hood. By the time we pulled into the Taco Johns in Tacoma it was clear the damage was serious. Charlie was struggling to remain calm and easy-going when Joe and his beautiful girlfriend Adrienne, met us at the fast food stop and led us to the townhouse they rented for a hefty sum.

The next morning we left the car with a mechanic, and enjoyed the company of Charlie's friends and the sights of the city. Our spirits were too high to be dampened when the mechanic called with bad news. Charlie's car was rare, and so were the parts. They were expensive, and had to be shipped from the other side of the country. Joe and Adrianne graciously encouraged us to extend our stay with them and so for nearly two weeks we lived on the periphery of their lives.

They were newly married, giddy in love, and watching them make dinner one night I yearned for their life. They had an adorable townhouse, a kitten, and a beautiful kitchen where they made all their meals from scratch. They were grownup. Stable. Happy. Smiling, I leaned into Charlie, heart full to bursting and whispered, "I want this." I could feel him bristle when he said, "I wasn't the one that did the leaving," and, without looking at me, followed Joe to the grill on the patio. I didn't bring it up again.

Several days later the mechanic called. The part was in and he would be able to have it replaced by tomorrow afternoon. The estimated total was well over half the money left in Charlie's stash, and he was not happy when he hung up the phone. We smoked our last cigarettes of the night in silence and the next morning packed up to wait out the day in the mechanic's shop. Joe and Adrianne had already been way more than gracious and needed to get back to their lives. We too were ready to move on and see more of the world than Tacoma had to offer - at least as much more as he could afford.

Afternoon was pushing into evening when the bill was finally paid and we again packed our bags around the woofer in the trunk. Charlie called Joe to thank him one more time, and we set off for Seattle. We were only a hundred miles outside Eugene when the little red coupe threw the U-joint. Charlie paid way too much for a tow to Eugene, we stayed way too long in a terrible little hotel waiting for parts - again - and we ate way too many meals at IHOP. We didn't even talk about looking for jobs; we had no interest in staying here. A week later– after many passionate rants on the phone with the mechanic in Tacoma – Charlie gave up and paid for the repairs. He now had just enough money to get us home, and maybe $100 more. We saw the very edge of the Redwood Forest at midnight before Charlie turned inland and began our 23-hour drive home.

**

I had missed my parents more than I had thought and they had been friendly and accepting when I had announced a couple of days before that I was coming home. After Charlie dropped me off, the three of us sat around the kitchen table talking about the trip, and all I had missed here. I told stories about seedy hotels and nightmares involving pancakes, they told tales of neighborhood parties gone awry and grandma's latest trip with her friends. And we laughed. I wistfully hoped I wouldn't have to answer the hard questions about why I had left school - and my job in Denver - what I had expected from my trip with Charlie and what I would do now.

I got my wish, mostly. They didn't ask those questions.

"You've gained a little weight," my mother said when we were alone in the kitchen, more an observation than judgment.

"Of course I have," I responded, only a little offended. "I just spent the last month sitting in a car, eating from fast food restaurants and IHOP."

"No," she said, gently. "You've always carried your weight around your hips. Your belly has gotten bigger. Are you pregnant?"

"NO!" I responded, incredulous, even as the tightness of fear squeezed my heart. I couldn't be pregnant. I was 19, unmarried and newly single, having again broken my relationship with Charlie, the only man with whom I had ever had sex - or ever loved. It couldn't be.

It could, of course, and that knowledge, or intuition, or maybe just the voice of my mother landed me in the checkout line at the tiniest, most out-of-the-way grocery store in town with a magazine to cover a little pink box. I silently begged the woman to hustle through the checkout process so I could hide the possibility my purchase suggested from any that might enter the store. I ignored the receipt, snatched my box and headed for the swinging door marked with a stick figure in a skirt. The bathroom was empty and I read the instructions carefully before I stuck the little plastic stick between my legs. The thin blue line appeared almost immediately. I sat for what felt like an hour staring at the thing as a hollow sense of reality wrapped itself around me. My heart was still beating but I felt nothing, thought nothing, saw nothing. I called Charlie from the pay phone in the grocery store lobby and asked him to meet me at the baseball fields on the edge of town.

My eyes were red and puffy by the time I dropped into the passenger seat of the little red car where I had spent the last month. I didn't know what to expect when I told him. He turned away, and stared ahead. I watched his profile carefully for a long while, and then Charlie dropped his head on the steering wheel and gripped it hard, shaking his head slowly.

It was not the response I had hoped for. I didn't know what I had hoped for until this very moment, until I saw his defeat. Suddenly I wanted him to put his arms around me and tell me it would be Ok... that we'd be OK. I wanted him to tell me that we'd get through this together, that he'd help take care of me, of us. Instead we sat in near silence for awhile, and then I went home to my parents.

I didn't tell my mother immediately, but when she asked again, a couple of days later I told her the truth and she put her arms around me assuring me it would be OK.

But it wasn't.

For days I lay in bed crying, sleeping, and fighting with God – why would you let this happen to me? I did not want to be a mother. What that hell am I supposed to do now?

A week later, when I could cry no more, a quiet acceptance settled over me and I pulled myself together. I got a job I was good at, with good benefits and good pay, that I did not love. Winter came to the mountains and as snow dusted the roads I surrendered myself to my place. I listened to the same 25 Christmas carols while I worked at the bank and came home to my parents house where I had dinner with the family, helped with dishes, played games or watched TV and went to bed. We laughed and joked and bonded. It was nice. It was simple, and routine... and nice. I bought a car that Charlie would like - one that was safe - and drove it to work and doctor appointments. I bought maternity pants and a breast pump. I spoiled my family at Christmas with gifts my new bank job easily paid for, but it was a life I could not love.

The Me I Was

My heart ached sometimes when I thought of the crummy little apartment I'd left in Brookings, my move to Denver and Peter's offer. Why had I thought I could have anything but a traditional life? Only the most incredible, talented people had lives outside of the ordinary. Everybody worked in jobs they couldn't love, to earn a sense of security that they could. I had let myself believe there for a minute that I could be different, that I could work doing things that made me happy and live a life I loved. I had been wrong. *I should never have gone to Denver*, I chastised myself. I should never have gotten the apartment or the dog.

But even as I tried to embrace the path I was on, the life I was about to live, I could not fully accept the idea of parenthood. It wasn't that I was afraid to do it alone, or that I was afraid to do it at all. But when I imagined my future as a mother it felt all wrong... like wearing a tight wool sweater against your skin on a hot summer day.

For some time I wondered if I were simply avoiding that which I "should" do, just like I had done with school and Charlie and the dog. I wondered if there was something wrong with me because I didn't want it, I wasn't excited about it, not even a little. Friends and family urged me along, assuring me that someday I would want to be a mother and the fact that I had started a little early would matter very little in the long run. I tried to imagine myself older, with children; happy, nurturing these precious little souls, and I could find no joy in it. There was another option... one that no one liked except me.

I stood in the shower one morning as the water cascaded down my back and ran my hand over my swollen belly praying. *Please, make the choice for me. I am too selfish to make this decision. Give me a clear sign. Tell me what you want me to do.* My desperation gave way to a moment of silence, and then a thought, loud in my mind, in a voice I was sure was not my own.

Give him up for adoption.

Immediately a weight lifted from me. The stress and worry about my future floated away as though I had let go of the string on a balloon. It was OK to do what I really wanted. I didn't have to feel selfish about it. It was meant to be this way, I was sure. The next day I made an appointment with a counselor at a local adoption agency.

***

Betty was a short, gentle woman with a radiant smile and thick brown hair.

"I don't want to choose the family," I told her almost immediately. "I think I would be judgmental and selfish. I want you to do it. I think you will make the right choice." She agreed to my plan and when we met thereafter, she did not speak of the family she had chosen. She told me nothing of her interviews with them, nothing of the preparations being made - legally and logistically, nothing of their excitement and joy. She told me I was brave - a suggestion I could not believe - asked me about my plans for my own future, and assured me I was still loved by God.

Late in the third trimester though, I had a quiet desire to know, to just see who they were. When I asked her to show me who she had chosen, she handed me a stack of profiles instead. "How about you just look through them and see which family you would choose. Then we'll look at who I chose and talk about it."

I leafed through the carefully crafted pages of hopeful fathers and mothers, read their stirring stories of the painful roads they had traveled and their belief that someday their child would come home to them. They all touched me, in some way, but one particular couple stood out. They lived just outside town in a modest home on a beautiful wooded lot. Exactly the kind of place I wanted to live someday. They were outdoorsy, spiritual and their enclosed photos gave me a sense that they were gentle, humble people and deeply in love. Exactly the kind of person I wanted to be someday. It seemed they could give my child the life he deserved, the life I would have wanted to give and knew I could not. My heart was warm and I loved them, somehow. When I set the rest of the stack aside, my counselor was grinning broadly. "That's the couple I chose," she said.

Jaclyn Lanae

FIVE

D r. Mitchell Kastr was just finishing his on-call shift when Dr. Simon rushed passed him in the hallway.

"We just got a call. Motorcycle accident. Doesn't sound good. Patient coded in the chopper. You'd better scrub in."

His young wife and new baby were home waiting for him and he had been looking forward to an early night. Bike week was always intense in the ER, but over the last day or so the traffic through the doors had finally slowed. He had hoped the serious cases were over. He pulled on gloves and a mask and pushed through the glass doors of the treatment room.

A young, blonde woman lay on the table and even through the deep purple bruises, he could see the trauma was extensive. Dr. Simon had taken the lead, and nurses were frantically dancing around the edges of the bed providing tools, towels, and supply kits. Others rushed in and out of the room bearing blankets, bottles of injectable medication, and a crash cart.

"One, two, three. Breathe!" a man pressing his palms against her sternum spoke as another covered the woman's mouth with a face mask attached to a plastic bottle and squeezed. "One, two, three. Breathe!"

"Six minutes." A nurse marked time for the CPR team.

"I need three more units oh-negative! NOW!" Dr. Simon shouted orders above the chaos.

"Internal bleeding is extensive," the head nurse hurriedly addressed the arriving doctor. "We've transfused six units already and still can't get any pressure.

"Both lungs are collapsed," Dr. Simon added. "Insert chest tubes, right and left side."

Dr. Kastr grabbed a scalpel and pressed it into the woman's flesh between her ribs making a small incision, then guided the pointed end of a plastic tube into the shriveled membrane, passing the tiny knife across the woman's chest to a nurse on the other side of the bed.

"Eight minutes!"

"Continue compressions!" Dr. Kastr barked.

One by one nurses stood back as they completed their tasks, unable to do anything more until the patient had a heartbeat.

All watched the heart monitor and compression team closely.

"Fluid drip is in" the head nurse stated, the last to step away. They all stood watching as life was forced into a purple-grey body.

The compression team continued. "Ten minutes."

"Doctor?" the head nurse said gently as she looked up at Dr. Simon. They all knew it was time to let her go. Much of the brain function had likely already been lost.

"Wait. We've got a beat! We've got a heart beat!" a nurse cried from the other side of the room. A quick cheer went up and the team went back to work. "Let's get her on the ventilator," Dr. Simon ordered, and several nurses began preparations.

Dr. Kastr began guiding a wide tube down the woman's throat while his colleague spoke. "She's still not holding pressure," he said with a somber, knowing look and turned to a nurse standing nearby. "Three more units O-negative on standby."

***

"Ok, Mom, but then I really have to go." Jess glanced longingly at her Jeep in the driveway and instead followed her mother upstairs to the den. She nodded, only half listening, as Lori read from the computer screen.

The Me I Was

"See? It says here gluten builds up in your system and can cause inflammation of all kinds. Inflammation causes pain and disease, so if you can get the gluten out of your diet you'll..." Jess just wanted to get out of there, retreat to the safety of her own home. She knew her mother's intentions were good... Through her own battle with a barrage of health issues Lori had discovered the healing power of food and had made it her mission to put this tool to use for the sake of her family's health. Jess, however, wasn't interested, not right now anyway.

The shrill ring of the phone on the desk startled them both. "Hello. This is Angie from Regional Hospital. Is Lori Thompson there?"

"This is."

"Ma'am, there's been an accident."

Jessi began to mouth to her mother that she had to go, collecting her keys and starting toward the door when Lori threw her hand up as a signal to stop, looking at her daughter with fear and fire in her eyes.

"What happened?" Lori spoke into the receiver.

Silence fell on the line.

"You'd just better come, ma'am."

Jess stood in the doorway, hand on the knob, chestnut brows knit together under the bill of her baseball cap and watched her mother's face with growing concern.

"Ok. We'll be right there," Lori said as she rummaged for her purse and hung up the phone.

"Get in the car!" she ordered. Jess could tell by the look in her eyes there was no room for questions. She hadn't even gotten her door shut before her mother put the vehicle in reverse and stomped on the gas, throwing both of them back in their seats.

"I just knew they were going to kill themselves on that thing," she said in a shrill voice. "I just knew it."

"What happened?" her daughter asked tentatively.

"Jaci and Trevor were in an accident," her mother responded, fear pitching her voice.

"Is she going to be OK?"

"I don't know. They wouldn't tell me anything!"

Several minutes later they finally pulled into the parking lot of the local hospital. "Park it and meet me inside," Lori instructed her youngest as she thrust the gearshift into park and opened her door.

The noise of the waiting room was a dull hum at the periphery of her consciousness when a nurse escorted her to a private room. Jess found her mother pacing, on the phone with a dear friend.

"Margie?"

"Hi Lori! How are..."

"Margie, I don't have time to talk. I'm at the hospital. Jaci's been in a motorcycle accident. I think it's bad." Her voice cracked and she could almost hear her friend become immediately and deeply concerned. "Start the prayer chains, will you?"

"Of course. Do you want me to come up there? How bad is it?"

"I don't know. I don't know anything. They wouldn't let me see her yet. I just called Father. He didn't answer. I think he's serving mass...."

"Are you the Thompsons?" the nurse spoke to the two women who had now been joined by a well dressed man with silver-blonde hair.

Lori nodded to the nurse and hung up without saying goodbye.

"Follow me."

Her father's steps were heavy in front of her as Jess followed the tiny train down the back hallway of the ICU past oversized trauma rooms; sterile, white and empty, waiting for the next patient. A flash of red caught her eye as they passed the last one and she slowed down to take another look.

The room was empty save for a blood spattered curtain that hung half way across the back wall. Whoever was in there must have died she thought. Then her breath caught in her chest. A familiar black leather jacket was dangling from a chair in the corner, a long reflective strip running down the sleeve.

***

Prayer books were strewn about. A few chairs and a lamp were all that saved the tiny room from life as a supplies closet. Silence was heavy between them and the tension was almost tangible. They glanced awkwardly at each other and then at blank walls and magazine covers, and back again. And they waited.

Eventually a short man in pale blue scrubs entered the room and addressed the family. "Dr. Kastr," he said, shaking each of their hands when they gave him their names, and then taking a seat on the very edge of an empty chair. He took a breath and exhaled quickly, but spoke in a calm, measured tone.

"It doesn't look good. She has broken nearly every bone on the left side of her body, some in multiple places. All eight ribs are broken and have collapsed both her lungs. The humerus and femur both have multiple fractures, her left knee is shattered, her pelvis and scapula are both cracked and the left ankle is badly dislocated. Her liver and spleen are lacerated, and there's extensive road rash on what remains of her legs…" he paused and took a breath. "Both of her legs have been nearly de-gloved. It means much of the skin and muscle has been pulled off, like a glove - or in this case, a sock - possibly from spinning tires." Lori's brown eyes were steady and she nodded, holding his gaze.

"She's lost a lot of blood," he continued. "She coded once in the helicopter on the way in and again here in the ICU. We've transfused 12 pints so far – her body probably only holds 7 or 8 - and her blood pressure has not stabilized." He looked them each in the eye, and then back at Lori. "I'm not confident we can save her life. I'm so sorry." He looked at the family with genuine sadness. "The body can only heal so much damage at one time… we can improve her chances - maybe give her a 50% chance of surviving this - if we amputate both her legs."

Lori, a petite woman with graying auburn hair, looked at the doctor for only a moment before asserting "You will save her life AND you will save her legs." The doctor watched her for a moment before standing to leave the room. When he had gone, Lori buried her face in her husband's chest and cried.

A short while later a nurse collected them and led them to a treatment room where they stood beside a vaguely familiar face, peeking out above heavy air-filled blankets. A layer of skin on her forehead and the end of her nose had been sheared off by asphalt, revealing raw and dirty flesh. She was sickly white, a paleness visible even as the bruises continued to develop under her tan, and swollen to thrice her normal size. An army of droning machines surrounded her bed, tubes and hoses running across her still body. Her eyes were closed and she looked simply asleep.

The nurse spoke gently. "She's in a drug-induced coma. It keeps her calm and free of pain. We'll keep doing everything we can, but it's likely she won't survive the night. It might be a good idea to..." she let her voice trail off. "I'm going to leave you for a bit, but we're right outside if you need anything."

Lori held her husband's hand and in the quiet of their hearts, the little family of three said goodbye.

SIX
2000

I thought I had found it there, in the second washed-out little college town I adopted as home, after settling my son into the arms of his rightful family. I enjoyed the school. I loved my roommate and our apartment. I adored my job. I had even found a collection of the people that quickly became the greatest friends I had ever had. I was in love, for the first time, and had a best friend I adored. Life in Laramie, Wyoming was good. At least it should have been.

I closed my Economics book, lit a cigarette and leaned back into a hundred-year-old, oversized window sill. Afternoon sun painted the windows of the buildings below and across from me a rich shade of gold. I stared at them for a long time, watching curls of smoke rise toward the open sky. What I wouldn't give, I thought, to lie down in the sun and just sleep. Forever.

I blinked, pulling my wandering mind back to reality, chastising myself for wishing away the life I had. I was just tired, I reasoned, knowing full well it was deeper than that. I was exhausted. And it wasn't from studying, or partying even. It was a different kind of exhausted. I was going to school because I thought I should, because I didn't know what else to do, but the education meant little to me. I was unremarkable in every way, broke, and to top it all off, the man I was in love with was not in love with me. Keeping hope alive – for anything – was almost more than I could do.

I blew out a drag through the screen and watched it float out over the sidewalk three stories below. Students had begun to congregate on the corners, talking and laughing, heading to the array of bars, restaurants and coffee shops that sat under or across from me. I stood up to call Devon when the phone rang. I grinned when I saw his name come up on the screen.

"I was just about to call you," I greeted him.

"Wanna go for a drive?" His voice was rich and sensual and I thought it matched his caramel colored skin.

"Yep."

Downstairs, I waited only a moment before he came around the corner in his 1984 Honda Accord.

Devon had been living in the plains of Wyoming much longer than I, and knew the roads around our little town like the back of his hand. He deftly maneuvered over wash board gravel and roads peppered with deep potholes as he told me about his day. His thick black hair stood off his head in perfect, springing curls that made me jealous, framing a face that was delicate, yet masculine. His eyes were the color of dark chocolate and soft now, telling me about the boy. Luke was a tall beauty, with jet black hair that he apparently left to its own devices. Devon had a sociology class with him, and had been pining after him all semester – and sharing every detail with me. But with Christmas break looming, he knew he would have to make his move or settle for hoping that fate brought them back together when classes resumed again in January.

"Tomorrow. I'm going to do it tomorrow," he asserted, thumping the meaty flesh of his palm against the steering wheel as if to literally drive the point home.

"What are you going to say?" I asked, watching prairie desert whip past as the road before us snaked a curve toward one of our favorite escapes; a place where the river turned and a sandy bank had been smoothed over the years to an almost beach-like quality.

"I don't know! What should I say?"

When he glanced at me I burst out laughing at his boyish insecurity and my heart softened to see him so vulnerable. He blushed behind his smile and turned back to the road. I suddenly thought I might have actually hurt his feelings with my laughter and tried to explain, still giggling.

"Devon! You really like this guy!" He gave me an incredulous look, as if to say 'What gave you the first clue?'

"I know, I know," I said "but you have to admit there have been a lot of interests..." Now he laughed, and it wasn't at all uncomfortable.

When we got to the place we called Sandy Hill and got out of the car, I lit a smoke and sat on the scrubby bank. He sat next to me, lit one of his own, and the smell of vanilla drifted toward me. I always saw him as such a delightful dichotomy. At once masculine and shy, with rugged good looks and a tender touch, a clean-eating hippy who smoked vanilla cigars more than I did cigarettes.

"How about you just give him a flyer and ask him to come to your show on Thursday?"

Devon dropped his hand over his knee, letting the slender cigar dangle between his fingers. "But I don't have flyers."

"So? You could make some." He nodded, letting himself be convinced. "You could even hand them out to a couple of other people in class so it didn't seem like you were just asking him."

"But what if he doesn't come because he thinks he's not important enough for me to ask specially?"

I grinned when I sighed. "Devon. You have to either nut-up and admit to this guy that you like him, or hope that he gets your vague messages and responds before you have no idea how to contact him."

"I know. I know." His turn to sigh.

The river before us was a muddy brown, perpetually churned up this time of year by cattle drinking at its banks, infrequent rain storms, and the incessant wind that dropped a fine dust into its waters. We watched it for awhile, making a runny clay out of its ingredients.

"So, what's with you and Kaleb?"

I turned to watch the meanderings of the river, and took a drag and a moment to work on my presentation.

"Eh," was all I could muster.

"Oh come on! You love him! Speaking of admitting things..." He gave me a wry look and I flashed him a smile before I looked back down the river and pulled through the tobacco again. "You've loved him FOREVER. Now you finally get together and all you can say is 'Eh'?"

I nodded without looking at him, knowing if I saw his face my eyes would well up and spill out and I'd have to tell him the whole truth. We'd been too close too long for him to let me ignore it, though, and when he pulled on my shoulder to get me to face him I could see the surprise in his eyes. I let him take me in for a moment before I hung my head between my knees and let the two tears that were now racing down my face land heavily in the dirt. I tried to wipe their evidence away on the shoulders of my shirt without him catching the motion but I was sure I had failed when I put the filter to my lips again. He waited patiently, and when I had composed myself and could stand the silence no longer, I told him. "He doesn't love me." Devon started to scoff, but I interrupted him. "No, don't do that. Don't try to make it better. You know Kaleb. He isn't just being standoffish. And he was never as interested in me as I was in him. And then there was the girl at the Cheese show..."

Devon was quiet now. He remembered the girl at the Cheese show... a magic little hippy woman with gorgeous long dreadlocks and a spunky attitude had met a friend of our crew the night before and ended up riding down to Denver with us for the concert. By the time we got there the friend and I sat together on the periphery of the dance floor and watched our respective partners have the time of their lives together. In that moment I had felt like I was in a soap opera, and wanted nothing more to do with Kaleb. Except that I was in love with him.

"I stopped calling or coming over. And he let me." Devon slid up next to me and held me to him while I fought back tears. "It's not just Kaleb," I said into his jacket. "It's the whole fucking thing. I'm exhausted. I have no idea what I'm doing here. I'm not like these people who have something they want to be, something they want to do. I have no idea... and no talent to build on... My job is just a college kid job - there's no future there. I don't even know what kind of job or future to dream about! I have great friends, but no real love... I can't see a happy future anywhere. I'm tired of putting on a happy face and hope is getting heavy. I don't even know why I'm going to school! I don't want to be a CEO or manager of a bank or anything. What the fuck am I getting a degree for?"

I finally pulled myself away and looked at him with a half-grin. He feigned hurt feelings. "No happiness anywhere, huh?" I smiled.

"Oh, there's happiness with you! But I can't take you with me."

He laughed and then joked about us getting married. "And Luke can be the pool boy! We'll move you down to Southern California with us and you can have a whole wing of the house and bring home as many men as you want." We laughed and Devon lit me another cigarette. "Kaleb doesn't deserve you anyway, if he doesn't know how amazing you are." His eyes softened when he caught my glance and he looked at me intently. "I'm serious. If they made a drug to make me not gay, you'd be the one." My heart melted and I kissed his cheek.

"Thanks, Devon. You always make it OK somehow." We both laughed, and then let the sound of the creek and the wind fill the space between us. "They don't though. So, I guess I'm going to have to slog through on my own." I grinned at him and we watched the sun drifting toward the horizon for a while before we got up and headed for his car.

***

Thursday classes were short for me and my afternoon lab was cancelled so I spent the morning at the coffee shop and the afternoon at Goodwill. It was a bright, cold autumn day and I relished in the sight and sound of leaves skittering across the parking lot as I carried my purchases to the old black Jeep that squatted half-way down the center row. You could almost feel the anticipation of the coming three day weekend in the air. Many professors had let their classes off easy, making Friday an option day. In fact I'd had only one professor that hadn't, but I knew my A in his class was not in jeopardy so I planned to take the day off anyway. It was almost like a little mini vacation for me. My excitement was brunted, though, by the knowledge I would likely spend most of it alone. Devon was going back to Cheyenne, Walter and the New Hampshire kids were going to Utah for a camping trip, Rachel, Emma, and crew were going to a show at Red Rocks. It was fine, I told myself – and meant it – I liked time alone. It was just that I wanted to be loved... I wanted to be really important to someone, and I wasn't. *Except Devon*, I thought with a half smile. It was a wicked irony, really, that he loved me as much as he did. He was absolutely gorgeous, incredibly talented, my very best friend... and gay. And I wasn't at all attracted to him – not sexually anyway. There was no chemistry. *Thank god*, I thought to myself. *Imagine the torture!* I shook my head as I climbed into the Wrangler. Yeah, that would be worse. Way worse.

I was excited for his show tonight, and not just because my best friend was a guitar prodigy. He made me feel special, even from the stage. I knew he sang to me because it was easier to look at me than at the crowd, and it was the perfect cover for love songs he'd really rather be singing to boys. But, it was Laramie, Wyoming, and so he sang to me. I loved it, of course, and was all the more thrilled when this beautiful man put his instrument down and came to have a drink with me during set breaks. Usually it was the whole crew; Walter, Carin and Cory from New Hampshire, Tess, Rachel and Emma, and Kaleb... and whomever any of them happened to be dating at the time. Tonight would be different, but good. Devon and I and would probably head up to Vedauwoo afterward and sit around the fire talking until we saw the sun, then head back to town for breakfast and bed. He'd leave for Cheyenne when he woke, but at least we'd have tonight.

The Jeep creaked with age as I eased her into the parking space behind my building. When I finally reached the top of four flights of ancient stairs, I could hear Tess on the phone with her mom through her bedroom wall into the hallway. Even after two years here I was still amazed at how thin the walls were. "Yeah, Ma, I'm almost packed. Trig gets out at 3:00 and I'll leave straight from there. Ya, I'm excited too. But I gotta go, Ma, I'm gonna be late for class." She was rolling her eyes at me and nodding into the phone. "Uh huh. Yeah, I will. I know where I'm going. I'll call you from the road." I giggled behind my hand and dropped my bags on the floor of my room. When I came back around the corner Tess was pulling a pink and white suitcase on wheels, carrying a studded hand bag and coffee, and hugged me with her sunglasses on. "Thanks so much for taking care of Brillo while I'm gone. I owe you one. Gotta run. Class starts in 5. See you Tuesday." She had long ago ended her hug and was still talking as she started down the stairs at the end of the hall. I smiled at her back and shook my head in amazement, quickly closing the door before Brillo the stealthy cat, could sneak out.

***

The light streaming through the small basement apartment window was soft and late, splashing all over the cluttered table and sink full of dishes. Rubbing my eyes I could feel the checkered pattern of the couch imprinted on my face, and the dew of sleep still clung to my cheeks. I started coffee and stopped by the bathroom before pouring myself a cup and donning a heavy sweater that was draped over the back of the couch. The morning sun did little to warm the concrete stairs down to Devon's apartment and I was grateful for the hat I had stashed in my purse before the concert last night and the heat of the coffee mug in my hands. I lit a cigarette and sipped delicately, soaking up the smell of fall in the air, the pile of leaves in the corner of the stairwell and some poorly carved pumpkins grinning at me from the balcony of apartments above and across the street from where I sat.

"I'm so glad you buy good coffee," I told Devon when he opened the door and wrapped his blanket tight around him. I recognized the comforter from his bed and grinned when he helped himself to the cup in my hands and took a drag of my smoke. We sat together for awhile, eye level with the street, sipping and smoking in silence. When I came back from refilling my mug and pouring one for him he held his blanket open and wrapped it around me. The gesture was kind and it was not uncomfortable when he pulled me close. "You OK?"

I knew exactly what he meant but feigned naivety anyway because I didn't really want to talk about it. "Yeah, of course, why wouldn't I be?" He shrugged and turned to face the street. "I saw Kaleb and Sasha come in last night." I nodded and stared ahead and let the silence become almost awkward before I turned to look at him.

"I know. I knew. I was pretty sure they'd been together since the show in Denver. It's fine. Honestly, seeing them together last night really finalized it for me. I think I am officially no longer in love with Kaleb." I looked away and could feel Devon staring at my temple.

"Ok," he said, still staring and sounding unconvinced.

"It was good. Really." I turned and looked him squarely in the eyes, and smiled. "Breakfast? Molinas?" He gave me one last squeeze and got up to go put proper clothes on. I lit another cigarette and sat for a while longer staring at the street.

***

Spring semester had started for me with a full roster of classes and a new job that paid more, but that I loved far less. By the time the season showed on the lilac bushes, I missed the coffee shop terribly and my attitude hovered on bitter when I was called in on my first day off after spring break. The mandatory training that ruined my Thursday was immediately redeemed though, when I was introduced to the new guy. His broad smile and bright blue eyes attracted me to him instantly. Devon, I knew, would not approve, but he'd accepted a last minute offer to live in Italy for a semester abroad, and it was only a few dinners and all-night walks passionately discussing God and politics before I was sure I was in love. Paul was brilliant, his father well connected in the politics of big business – even from his desk in Montana - and the two together made for impassioned conversations about government, society, humanity and our role in the whole hot mess.

The June wedding was small and very simple. It was also probably in part, my first and most real act of rebellion. We moved out of my downtown apartment into an adorable little rental on the wrong side of town, adopted two dogs and a cat, and almost immediately everything began to fall apart. I was only a day late getting my form to the registrar, formally withdrawing from my fall classes, but it was too late and I would only be issued a partial refund. It felt like the smack my father would have given me if he was that kind of man, and if he knew what I had decided to do.

It had nothing to do with Paul – almost nothing anyway. Something in the way I saw myself had changed. I wasn't just taking the appropriate steps and hoping what I wanted would be gifted to me when I got to where I was supposed to be. I was diverging from the path – from the prescription life - and I liked it. It certainly wasn't comfortable, far from it, but it felt... grown up. Besides, I rationalized, I wouldn't love my life in a corner office anyway. I didn't want to be a business woman – I wanted to be ... well, I didn't know yet. But something else.

Our new relationship required one of us to leave the company and my new job was not going well. We were broke, in every sense of the word. After several months of reveling in bucking the system, the delusion perpetuated by easy access to too much marijuana and cheap cigarettes, the reality of the place I now was, the place I had really chosen for myself, was beginning to sink in.

I was sure Devon was angry when he called one brisk fall afternoon and asked me to go for a drive. I agreed anyway, mostly because I had missed him terribly.

"So, married, huh?" he asked almost immediately and without looking at me.

"It was magic."

"What, the wedding?"

"No, the dating." He still wouldn't look at me, but I could feel him soften so I explained. "He thought I was beautiful – and told me so... he covered shifts at work so I could go home for Jess's birthday... he even called the power company to pay my bill for me and got them to drop the late fee. We took long walks every night, talking... and he was such a good kisser." Devon finally looked at me.

"Was?" I looked down and took a drag of my cigarette, then shrugged.

"I dunno, D... something changed. Like, right after the wedding. He started calling in sick to work all the time, then when they got this new girl he started picking up extra shifts..." Devon pulled his Accord to the side of the road, shut it off and lit a smoke.

"You think he's cheating on you?"

"No. In fact I'm pretty sure he isn't. But that almost makes it worse. It's not about sex. It's about love. She has a kid... I think he wants to take care of her. I think he likes to be the hero and he doesn't want to be mine anymore." I didn't cry because I couldn't, I had cried all the tears before.

"What'd Kaleb say?"

I laughed bitterly. "He wanted me to come back."

"Why didn't you? You loved that guy."

"Devon, the thing is, he didn't love me. And even if we got back together and he finally did, I'd never be anything more than the woman he grew to love. I want a man to just flat out love me. Like, I-can't-live-without-you kind of love."

"And Paul gives you that?" I could tell he was angry, his words almost sarcastic, and I knew I kind of deserved it.

"Nope. Not anymore." The quiet between us seemed almost to pull the angry out of us both and we sat there for awhile staring at the long-abandoned dirt road in front of us that disappeared into the folds of a pair of small hills.

"Why? Why do these men come into my life only to fall in love with someone else as soon as we get to 'good'? What's wrong with me?" Devon looked at me with compassion.

"There's nothing wrong with you. It's them."

"Ppppffffttthhhhh. Right. That's what everybody says, but there's always something about a person that makes them attract a certain kind of man or woman. If I were truly anything special, they'd stay."

"Bullshit!" Devon's voice was so close to angry that I turned to him in surprise. "Sorry. But seriously. Bullshit. You're pretty, and sweet... That dread-y chick Kaleb went for wasn't nearly as cute as you are. And I heard she's kind of a bitch."

My turn to call bullshit. "Not only was she beautiful; tall and skinny... but she's an artist. A good one. Shit, if I were gay, I'd be in love with her. She's exactly the kind of woman I'd like to be. And she was nice enough to me..."

"And I don't know this Sarah girl Paul is after, but I'm betting the same is true for her." I shook my head.

"Nope. She's gorgeous. Thick dark hair, bright blue eyes... really sweet and funny.... Thanks for trying to make me feel better though." I looked at him to punctuate my sincerity. "The thing with Sarah is, I'm pretty sure it's not even just that she's beautiful. It's that she needs him or something. But I do too! Right?" Devon gave me a half smile and shrugged.

"So what're you gonna do?" I sighed and turned to stare out the window. "We're talking about moving back to Rapid City... making a fresh start there." He looked at me expectantly. "We can stay with my parents until we get jobs, get back on our feet..." I could feel him watching me and I knew what he wanted. "I just want to get through it. Then I'll figure the real stuff out." I paused to take a drag. "So, how was Italy?" I asked, turning to smile at him, desperate for a topic we could enjoy. "It was good. Except that when I got back my best friend was married."

***

I got a job at a doctor's office and after spending a month or so with my parents, we rented a little house in a no-collar neighborhood on the west side of town. Paul took work for a delivery service and we struggled on. We didn't even fight much, but the space between us was planets apart.

He had called in again this morning, playing off his raspy too-many-cigarettes-last-night voice as the flu, and I was using my time in the car on the way to work to wallow in my self pity, analyze what I felt, and feed my anger and disappointment with all the reasons I had to be mad at him. He wasn't the man I had married. Not by a long shot. I felt deceived, frustrated, and exhausted. *I'm one of those women,* I thought, *the ones who spend their whole life just barely holding everything together and taking care of the deadbeat on the couch.* I immediately felt bad for thinking it of him, but the sting of bitter truth was sharp. I could almost feel a wall go up when the realization hit me; I asked for this. This is the life I chose. I steeled myself with the implication - this is the life I would have to live.

I wouldn't be happy. Not like I had thought I would. I wouldn't have a career I loved, and I wouldn't have a passionate, loving, relationship and truly beautiful marriage either. I could make the best of it - I'd have to. Lots of people did. I just needed to accept my position and let go of the idyllic little world I had been dreaming of. What had I thought it would be like, anyway? I'd marry a magic man and suddenly everything would be OK? I guessed I had, and I had been wrong. This was reality, and the reality was those kinds of lives existed for very few. I'd spend my life taking work doing whatever I could to pay the bills, come home to a man that liked me but was not in love, and live the same day everyday until I died.

It was a quiet acceptance that had settled over me by the time I put my car in park and joined the rest of the office staff in the big room at the back of the building. The lead Chiropractor had invited a counselor, a healer, named Marianne, to meet with us today as a last ditch effort to move us through and past the dysfunctional office environment that was growing more toxic every day. Stress was largely to blame, the spilling over of personal lives into office dynamics, and too few patients to pay too few employees to do too much work, had culminated in a space that felt both stagnant and on the verge of disaster all the time. The tension, the silent fighting had reached a fever pitch and was so apparent customers had begun to see it. All of us were always on the brink of breaking down.

Marianne instructed us to sit in a circle while she readied some things, and when she turned around she broke out in laughter. "Wow. What do you guys have going on here?" She gestured to our circle.

We had pulled our chairs up so closely that our knees were nearly touching. The room was at least 1100 square feet and there were five of us. We all looked around at each other, startled by the realization and laughed nervously to make light of it. She had us pull our chairs further out, stretching the circle. I literally and immediately felt a weight lift from me. We all did.

We had gotten close in the months we worked together, and while the environment was fun at first, the mood had quickly turned tense. Each of us was in a major stage of our personal lives, and the office as a whole was endeavoring to overcome the challenges of a brand-new practice and simultaneously establish itself as a beacon of health in the community. We had narrowed our scope to a single possibility; stick together and keep moving forward whether it was good for us or not. The rest of the session we worked as a group on our individual issues and an hour later emerged from the big room all feeling empowered and much more independent.

On my way home that night I remembered the thought I had that morning and came to a completely different conclusion; I deserved happiness. If we really did only get this one life, I wanted to spend it as filled with joy as possible. If he wasn't right for me, I probably wasn't right for him. Holding onto this marriage was only keeping us both from real happiness, and we were only doing it because we didn't want to be embarrassed, we didn't want to be wrong. We were each looking for something in the other that neither of us could give. The hopelessness and surrender of the morning had turned to conviction. I had to do something different.

A week later I had convinced a friend of mine to give me a ride to Custer, an adorable little tourist town in the southern Hills where I thought I might find a job. I needed space, I needed perspective, I needed to be alone.

I ate breakfast on the porch of our little rental house that morning while Paul slept, and let the spring sun warm my face. I closed my eyes and breathed deep, desperation pushing on my heart. I reached out to a higher power I couldn't define and felt the desire in the center of my soul. *Ok, if this is what I'm supposed to do, if leaving Paul is the right thing for me, I need to find a job, today, and a place to live. With my dog. For free.* I immediately recognized the sinking feeling when I really understood what I was asking for. *Please*, I begged, *I need a new start. If this is truly what my soul wants, make it easy.*

When we got to the sleepy little town, I walked into every shop on the single downtown street. One by one they told me that they had done their hiring for the season. My heart sunk as I worked my way further and further down the sidewalk until I could see the very last door. I knew this was my last chance. My only chance. Just getting a ride out here hadn't been easy, and I needed a job. Now.

The Me I Was

The last little antique store on the eastern edge of Main Street had me waiting at a table outside for the manager, a gruff-looking old fellow with a belly that stuck out far past his toes. When he sat down across from me I was intimidated, almost to the point of telling him never-mind and running off down the street. Instead, I burst forth with my story, my nerves spurning me to reveal more than I had meant to; that I was trying to get out of a marriage I should never have gotten into, that I had literally not a penny to my name and nowhere to live, and a dog, and did he have work for me? He frowned when he looked at me.

"I jus' went through a divorce myself," he said slowly. "You got any retail experience?" I told him yes, that I had worked for a ski and snowboard shop when I was a kid, and in a coffee shop for quite awhile in college. He looked at me a little sideways for a long minute, and then said, "You're hired." I felt a weight lift from me and my heart rejoiced. And then sank.

"Thank you," I said, trying to sounds as excited as I had been a moment before. "Thank you so much! There's just one other thing... do you know where I could stay for awhile until I get on my feet?"

He nodded, rather without smiling, and said, "I got a cabin a mile and a half east. You can stay there."

"Oh, thank you! But I really have no money. I couldn't pay you for..." He held up his fat, gnarled hand.

"No need. I let temp help live in 'em for the summer sometimes. Ain't nice enough to rent to tourists, but it's a dry place to sleep and has a sink for washing." I was elated.

"And my dog?"

He nodded only a little begrudgingly. "Can't hurt anything in there, I guess."

I put in my notice at the doctor's office and my friend gave me a ride to the one room cabin with water that came from a hand pump where I'd be staying with my dog and the cat and my clothes.

I wanted to see if watching me - and our relationship - slip through his fingers would be enough to spawn change. It wasn't, not really, anyway. As tourist season drew to a close I packed up what I had and moved back to Rapid City to see if we could make it work, but it didn't last long.

He had stopped working all together and by the time I got home, he'd been fired. Our only car had broken down, our bills weren't paid, and shortly after I arrived he was evicted from the home we had been renting and the cat ran away. My courage finally caught up to my decision when he showed up really drunk one night and threatened me. The next morning I called my Mom. She picked me up from the friend's house where we had been living on the floor with both our dogs and all our worldly possessions and I never went back.

After two years of marriage I asked for a separation. We both knew it was just the politically correct step before an inevitable divorce. There were a lot of reasons, but for me the truth was simple; we weren't meant for each other. Several weeks later I started a new life and a new job – at the local motorcycle dealership.

SEVEN

Thin clouds were blushing with dawn when Dr. Kastr stripped himself of his bloodied gloves. He had spent the last eight hours picking dirt and gravel from the shreds of what had once been muscled legs, and there was still a lot to do. If she made it through the next 8 hours, he would begin again tomorrow.

Dr. Simon came in to survey the progress and update the prognosis, gently picking up a section of flesh part way down the left shin and peeling the skin back, laying the flesh of the knee cap on the thigh while he inspected the freshly scrubbed tissue. "You've done a good job here, Doctor," he said "but I have to ask why."

Dr. Kastr's eyes were heavy with exhaustion and defeat. "The family wants us to try to save her legs," he told his colleague. "I've been debriding them all night." The bloody tweezers still had tiny chunks of dirt stuck to the pointed tips when he dropped them into the autoclave tray.

Dr. Simon shook his balding head. "Even if we can save her legs, she'll never walk again. She has a much better chance of survival if we amputate."

Dr. Kastr nodded. "I told them that. Her mother is certain she will survive – and walk." Dr. Simon gave his friend a look that was both incredulous and sad, and they both stared at the patient a moment before moving into the next room to clean up. "Honestly, Simon, I'd be surprised if she survived the night. She's still losing blood. We've transfused 20 pints and there's still no pressure. She's teetering."

Jaclyn Lanae

EIGHT

Word of the accident spread quickly among friends and when Marianne heard the news she immediately went to the hospital to visit her friend. Many others who had done the same crowded the waiting room, having heard the same compassionate but firm response from the receptionist's desk; "Sorry, immediate family only." Undeterred, Marianne went home to connect with her friend in a different way.

The house was quiet, and she was alone. She got comfortable in her favorite chair, closed her eyes, took a few breaths to quiet her mind, and then reached out from her heart. Jaci quickly appeared before her, sitting on a stool in jeans and a t-shirt, long blonde hair falling loosely down her back and with a warm smile on her face. A wide band of blue light surrounded her and she smiled at Marianne, peaceful and deeply happy. They greeted each other and spoke for a moment before Marianne said "Jaci, if you want to heal, you have to let that light in. Those are prayers, and you will need them if you are going to get through this."

"I don't know if I'm coming back." she replied, slow and calm. "It is so beautiful here, so peaceful. Everything is perfect and comfortable. There is light and warmth and I can just rest. I don't think I want to survive this. I don't want to go through it. It will hurt so much."

Marianne was surprised, at first, but knew the soul of her friend knew its own destiny. "Of course you know what is best," she said. "Think about letting those prayers in anyway. They will only help you, whatever you decide." "I love you," Marianne said before she said goodbye, sure her friend would never return to this world.

***

Casseroles piled up in the freezer at home and the family of three passed their time in the waiting room. No change, no news, nothing. She still wasn't breathing on her own, she still couldn't hold blood pressure, and she still wasn't healing. She was dying. Hundreds came with food, and cards and tearful hugs. Many held their hands in prayer. Hope waned as they watched first one sunrise and then another pass. Eventually they would have to accept that she wasn't going to make it and let her go, and the time was quickly coming. Handshakes and long hugs, phone calls and hours on bent knees quickened the clock for Mother and Father, but the younger child kept to herself. She engrossed herself in puzzles, looking up just long enough to smile and thank the strangers that patted her back offering grim-faced condolences.

On the third day, an exhausted Dr. Kastr came into the waiting room the family had adopted as home with a weak smile. "Good news. Her heart beat this morning was much closer to normal and her blood pressure has improved. The transfusions are holding. We're not sure why, but she's stabilizing." All three nodded. A mixture of relief and pensive hope seeped into the room. "And so far her legs look ok – no infections or major tissue death. We won't have to amputate as long as that remains true. If she continues to improve, we can take the ventilator and chest tubes out later this week or early next. We're going to keep her in the coma for now, though. There's still a lot of damage to be repaired." He paused and looked at them again. "It's important we be realistic about this. She likely won't ever walk again. But, she does have a better chance of surviving."

Weak smiles and quick nods were shared around the room. Jess sat quietly in the corner, a smile in her heart. The doctor's news was not a surprise. She hadn't expected it to take this long, but she knew her sister would survive.

She had to.

The Me I Was

There had been a point, that first day, when she had been afraid. She had left the hospital late, with a bag containing a torn leather jacket, a small collection of rings and a pair of mutilated jeans, still bearing the blood and hamburgered flesh of her older sibling. At home, with the contents spread out before her on a towel, the cold reality had washed over her and she had cried out silently, tears streaming down her face and her chest heaving to catch a breath. 'Jaci! What did you do to yourself?' Her love for her sister poured forth in her tears, exposed in its depth by the possibility that she would soon be standing by the grave of her best friend in the whole world. When the sobbing finally subsided, helplessness took the place of fear and she absently fingered the buckle of her sister's belt, sticky pink tissue still lodged in the hollow spaces. *I have to clean it*, she thought. *She'll want it when she gets out.* So, for the next four hours, armed with cotton swabs and hydrogen peroxide, she'd cleaned.

***

"You have to keep her calm," nurses warned as they led her down the hallway. "She's in a coma so she won't be able to talk to you, but she can hear you. Talk to her. Just don't do anything to excite her."

Jess nodded.

A quiet humming, punctuated by the soft sucking of the oxygen tank emanated from the army of medical equipment stationed around the oversized white bed. Her sister's head was turned slightly to the side – and except for the collection of hoses strung all over the bed – she looked as though she were sleeping. Jess stared at her for a long time.

They had fought, about everything as little girls do, but now, as her eyes wandered over a body swollen and black from bruises, she was looking at her friend. Her heart ached and she willed those green eyes to flutter open, look at her and smile. Nothing, no sound but the measured tones of the heart monitor illustrating her sister's delicate hold on life.

Avoiding the web of tubes she slipped her hand into her sibling's and squeezed it gently. "Hi Jaci. It's me. I'm here," she whispered. Heavy silence responded, laced with that quiet hum.

She watched her sister's chest rise and fall ever so slightly. For a long time she just looked at her. Memories of their youth and their battles - and now their adulthood and friendship – flickered through her mind. *Please*, she begged, *please be ok.*

She shook her head fighting tears and looked again at the patient wrapped in blankets and swollen nearly beyond recognition. She squeezed a limp hand, tears stinging behind her eyes, and looked into her sister's face.

"You can't leave me here," she whispered desperately.

Instantly monitors squealed and alarms rang out. The line on the blood pressure monitor spiked again and again, her sister's eyes fluttered and she surged against the restraints. Terrified, Jess fled the room as nursing staff ran in.

The Me I Was

NINE

Everything was fuzzy. A thin reality cloaked in softness induced by heavy doses of morphine. I had dreamt of my job, my apartment and my mother in a bright shade of green. I opened my eyes for the first time to the sight of an attractive young man standing at the foot of my bed dressed in blue scrubs and holding a clipboard.

I smiled and attempted conversation but the words tumbled out of my mouth awkwardly. He furrowed his brow and went back to his charts.

"Someone is here to see you," he said stoically, hanging the clipboard off the end of my bed. A moment later a familiar face pushed through the door.

"Mom! Hi! I knew you'd be wearing that color." I gushed, eyes stinging with tears I didn't understand. "I just had the most amazing dream! I want to redecorate my apartment. I'm thinking I could get some old suitcases and stack them by the front door. I could use them for storage too...

She smiled, but there was a tension, a sadness in her eyes. Something was different, something was wrong but I could not make sense of it and it didn't seem important to try. I knew time had passed, but I had no idea how much or why I had been asleep, and she didn't say. It never occurred to me to ask. She held my hand for awhile and left me to my room and my thoughts. As the door slowly swung closed behind her, I asked her to call Jensen and tell him I wouldn't be in today.

When I woke the second time I was less fuzzy - though not by much - and took stock of my surroundings. The trees outside the window reminded me of the school where Jess had spent all of her junior high and high school years. It was a beautiful, modern brick building next to the cathedral, and across from the hospital. *That must be where I am. I must be in the hospital.* The realization stirred something in me but a moment later it was gone.

I slept and woke again several times, vaguely aware of someone washing my hair and various people writing on clipboards. After two weeks in the ICU and two days pulling out of the coma, I was moved to the tenth floor. I'm sure I nodded when the nurses told me, but the announcement had no meaning and, still numb, it didn't matter. When they came to get me, though, I was afraid. Of what I had no idea, but I knew that I did not want to be moved. I bit my lip and watched the ceiling tiles pass above me as a small team of nurses wheeled my bed and army of machines to the elevator. They attempted to strike up conversation with me but even as I realized I would normally have chatted right along with them, I could bring myself to respond with nothing more than grunts and weak smiles.

The room was large, the walls painted the color of coffee with too much cream, and I thought it did little to soften the sterile feeling. It still felt like a hospital, and the air stunk of sickness and death. I had the room to myself, at least, with a view of the leaves turning yellow on the trees beyond the parking lot and for the next several weeks my entire world was contained within.

Reality returned quickly, and painfully. My left arm hung limp at my side, a long seam stretching from pit to elbow where a plate had been used to hold the splintered bones in place. A matching scar ran from the middle of my left thigh through my knee for the same reason. Foot-long screws were twisted through the flesh of my right leg and into the bone, supports for the halo like device called an External Fixator, holding my leg rigid, and a matching line of holes ran down the left side where one had already been removed. The worst, though, was my legs themselves. Gaping holes lay open in the flesh of both. The tissue on the left had been shredded away so completely Doctor Kastr could fit three of his fingers under the shin bone. What remained was saved from completely peeling down my calf by a couple of inches of intact skin behind and below my knee. Just beneath the front of my right knee and wrapping around the calf was another shallow hole about the size of my father's hand where tires, presumably, had shredded the flesh and torn the femoral artery. What skin remained was peppered with deep patches of road rash.

I never fully understood my condition and never really found a need to ask. Something had happened. Now I was here and it hurt and I just wanted it to all be over. I felt empty. Almost disinterested in what was happening and why. The hollow feeling of my youth was back, intensely magnified by the pain and my captive state.

I ignored it as much as I could, or drowned it out with cable TV and the morphine pump. I became a student of home design and fashion, finding solace in HGTV and the DIY channel. Days were filled with doctors and nurses, coming and going every few hours. They asked about my pain, told me about the next steps in the process, ran tests, and took blood samples. Lots and lots of blood samples. I watched TV, talked just enough with visitors not to be rude, and watched the clock.

Nights were long and rest did not come easily. Finding enough comfort for sleep was hard, especially with the monstrous Fixator. I devised elaborate pillow designs to trick my body into thinking I was lying on my side, delayed using the morphine pump until I could bear it no longer, tried every possible bed position but nothing really worked. I was antsy, unable to rest in part because I didn't need it. My body wasn't tired. It was useless. Even when I could find a tolerable amount of comfort, I was interrupted every couple of hours for blood samples. In the relative quiet between such visits, when nothing was on TV, I could not ignore the heartache and my mind would not be still.

***

"She will likely be in the hospital until Christmas," Dr Simon warned, turning sideways in the plastic waiting room chair so he could face the family. "She's improving, but there will be setbacks. You just can't avoid it with this much damage. Infections, colds... her body is working so hard to heal and process all the meds, it can't fight off every little bug too."

"What about her legs?" Lori asked.

"We're leaving the wounds on her legs open for a little while. They'll actually re-build some of the lost tissue on their own, if we can keep the existing tissue - and her whole body in general - healthy. The more her body can heal itself, the stronger, and more normal she'll be when it's over. It does leave them open to infection - but with diligent cleaning, it is a risk worth taking. The Wound Care Team will be in later today and you'll see how it works." The silver in their hair had spread, it seemed, just in the last few weeks and reflected the fluorescent light when they nodded.

He shifted uncomfortably in his seat and a short silence settled in the room. "I want to make sure you understand... she might be able to keep her legs, but she won't walk again. And there is still a possibility that we may have to amputate. Either way it's probably a good idea to start looking into home modifications, or..." he let his voice trail off, gave them both a compassionate smile, and left the room. Lori looked at her husband. "What about her apartment? All those stairs!" He nodded and patted her knee. "I know. We'll talk about that later. Let's just see what happens, OK?" She nodded and rested her head on his shoulder, fighting back tears.

***

My mother had taken it upon herself to prepare every meal for me - tailor made for healing; no flour, absolutely no sugar, and very little salt. Just food. Fruits, vegetables and high

76

quality protein. She had just finished begging me to eat one more bite of the chicken and veggies she had so lovingly prepared when two chipper young nurses entered the room pushing a metal cart. They smiled brightly when they introduced themselves and I liked them immediately. They chatted idly with my parents and me about weather and news and the interior design show on TV as they laid out their supplies; gauze, lots of clean towels, small sheets of something that looked like black foam, a stiff bristled brush, and a machine that resembled a giant water-pik. "You got extra Percoset and Vicodin this morning, right?" the woman who had introduced herself as Karen asked. I shrugged. My mother checked with the nurses station and confirmed I'd been given the extra pills. Karen nodded. "And you've got the morphine pump... that should help." I was confused but too apathetic to ask questions.

"Dr. Simon spoke to you about keeping the wounds in her legs open, right?" she addressed my parents. They nodded together. "So what we're going to do is scrub the exposed tissue really, really well. Then we'll cut this foam to fit the wounds," the other woman, Tudi, held up a piece in example "and lay them on top. Then we attach a hose to the top of the foam with tape, and connect it to the Wound V.A.C.," Tudi gestured to a machine about the size of a car battery, "which works just like it sounds... it sucks fluid out of the wounds around the clock. That – hopefully – will keep her from getting any infections." We all nodded stupidly, only kind of understanding.

"This," Tudi said as she held up a blocky machine "is like a supersized waterpik. We use it to spray a saline solution into the tissue while we scrub. Karen picked up what was apparently some kind of soap and a stiff bristled brush. "You might want to give yourself an extra dose of morphine," she said. I did as she suggested and she turned on the waterpik. As soon as the intense stream of saline hit the last of the muscle in my leg I felt an ice cold pain shoot up my leg. The pain was so intense I thought I might well go into shock and genuinely hoped for it. Then Karen began with the brush.

The two scrubbed the open, hamburgered flesh - nerves and all - vigorously, and I fought a losing battle with the stream of tears running down my temples and into my hair. Mother and Father each took a hand. I squeezed as tight as I could and forced myself to breathe. A half hour later the brush and waterpik were laid aside and I exhaled in relief. It was over. Karen and Tudi were cutting pieces of foam to fit each of the holes, taping it down and attaching the hose.

"You did really, really well, honey," Tudi told me with a smile as she packed up the cart. "You just let your nurse know if you want more Percoset next time." I shot my dad a horrified glance.

"They have to clean them regularly, sweetheart," he said, leaning over the edge of my bed. "If we can keep your legs clean, you have a better chance of keeping them. So the Wound Care Team will be coming every few days to clean them and change the foam and hoses."

"Every other day." Karen corrected him. I stared at them absently and for a brief moment considered asking my doctors to just go ahead and cut my legs off. Instead I nodded and tried to smile when they said goodbye, only mostly aware of what was going on. When I closed my eyes I slept more soundly than I had since I had come out of the coma, and for the next month, that was the reward that got me through the cleanings.

***

The hue and angle of the sun outside my windows spoke of September. A nurse with a round face and wide smile stood at the foot of my bed, clipboard in hand, scribbling down readings from various machines, chattering away in a thick southern accent.

"Lovely mornin' out there... after all those storms last night. My heavens that thunder was loud! Some my patients had a hard time sleepin'. You did too, didn't ya honey? Wish I coulda..." she paused mid sentence to look up at me. "Good news, honey," she said with a broad smile. "You gonna get to go outside today! Ain't that excitin'?"

My heart sank and my stomach twisted. I obliged her with a smile. "Excitin'" wasn't quite the word I would have used. She chattered on then dropped my chart at the end of the bed, the scent of sterilizing lotion lingering in the air behind her when she left.

Every time I had been moved from my new little world, fear filled me. Not just worry, but full-on fear. Nearly every day there was something I had to be wheeled downstairs for... a trip to Xray, another procedure or surgery... and every time I was scared. Even the surgeries I wanted – like the impending skin grafts that would close the holes in my legs, allowing me to go home – filled me with dread and I had no idea why. I turned up House Hunters and let myself dream of a beautiful home and a normal life, and ignored the impending horror.

I did not have long with the emotion, or the remote, when my parents arrived with a barrage of nurses that collected at the end of the bed. They spoke in hushed tones and gestures, pointing at the clipboard that hung on the footboard. Mom and Dad came to stand beside me and Mom took my hand. She asked me how I slept, told me there would be no cleanings today, and talked about 'outside' as though I should be thrilled. I would have been – before. The "Mobilization Team" stood at the end of my bed, beaming.

I would rather have stayed in bed for *Design on a Dime*, but it was clearly a big deal and I was clearly supposed to be happy about it so I smiled. A wheelchair was pulled to the side of the bed and the nurse that delivered it looked at me expectantly. The chasm between my bed and the chair seemed impossible to span and for a moment, I thought of telling them it was OK, I didn't need to go outside. My mother's hopeful face, though, gave me pause and a moment later instructions were flung from one side of the bed to the other.

"Let's get her on her side," I heard them say quietly, speaking to one another as though they were planning a hostile takeover.

"Try rolling on your side," I was instructed loudly.

I began the effort and it was immediately obvious that course of action would do nothing toward our end goal. The External Fixator made "rolling" of any kind impossible. I looked up at the nurse that appeared to be leading the charge with a question in my eyes, and a weary smile.

"Ok, well, let's just get you turned around. Face the side of the bed and we'll go from there."

I set my left arm in my lap, and looked around my body. I figured I could sort of shuffle the cheeks of my butt to scootch and drag my legs to the edge of the bed. So I pushed myself up with my right arm and twisted toward it, then dropped myself to the mattress, leaned back, scootched, drug and swung, then pushed myself up and started the process again. Beads of sweat were forming on my forehead when I finally completed the task but I had done it. My right leg stuck straight out, held rigid by its halo-like Fixator. The left – still casted from the ankle down – hung almost normally over the edge. The Wound V.A.C. beeped loudly at the foot of the wheelchair where it had been temporarily relocated for the excursion, indicating one of the tubes had come loose from the foam padding.

I took a few deep breaths as the staff bustled about correcting the problem, successfully avoiding the eyes of my parents. It was more movement than I had experienced in well over a month and it hurt. Badly. I was exhausted already. I didn't like it. Any of it. I was embarrassed in front of myself by my desire to repeat the whole thing in reverse and switch on HGTV again. Instead I pushed the thought out of my mind and steeled my resolve. A few feet of medical tape later, the beeping stopped and the room was almost quiet. I looked up at the faces around me, awaiting instruction.

"Ok," a male nurse was taking charge. "Samantha, you hold the wheelchair as close to the bed as you can, just behind her. Once she's up, make sure she doesn't put any pressure on that cast. She should be able to make a half turn on the right leg and sit down." Everyone acknowledged understanding of the plan with a nod, myself included.

"All right. Let's get her standing then."

The prospect was daunting. Five screws, each nearly a foot long were twisted through the flesh of my thigh and calf, and into the bone to hold the Fixator in place. My right leg was essentially a giant, steel-reinforced toothpick. I'd really have to more tip myself onto it than actually stand, but it seemed feasible, and that was more than it had been a few minutes ago.

I teetered on the edge of the bed for a moment, my tongue pushed out between my lips in concentration, looking down at my stiff leg, my mind caught between knowing what to do and understanding it couldn't be done. What I wanted to do was bend my knee. What I needed to do was push myself on top of my stiff leg and balance for a moment, without putting any pressure on my left leg, and without the use of my left arm. I felt like a gymnast preparing for a vault routine. I rocked forward, then back, then forward, then back, then launch!

I hadn't taken into account that my right arm was, of course, shorter than my leg and therefore not long enough to push me fully upright. As I started to fall back onto the bed everyone in the room sucked in a collective breath, reaching out as though they could catch me, before exhaling as I landed with a soft thump on the mattress. I looked up at them and grinned, knowing what a sight this must be. Everyone smiled back at me. I knew if my sister were here she would have burst out in laughter but the feeling in the room was that of pity and I desperately wished she were there.

A nurse positioned herself across the wheelchair from me, arms outstretched as a mother beckoning their child to risk his first steps.

"OK, let's try again."

I breathed deep, sucking in willpower, made eye contact with the nurse and launched up again, this time grabbing her outstretched hand. Success!

Searing pain shot up and down my right leg, the weight of my body born entirely on the long screws and muscles that had not been called to task in over a month, and in that same moment a sense of accomplishment and excitement washed over me. I was standing. I would have cried at the intensity of the emotion were it not for the physical pain. My father and I locked eyes and the entirety of understanding passed between us. I felt his relief, joy and pride. And I knew when I saw the mist in his grey-blue eyes that he felt my pain, but also knew my glory.

I made a quarter hop-turn on my peg leg and literally collapsed into the wheelchair. The pain subsided. I smiled, and I almost meant it. The IV pole was rigged to accommodate the Wound V.A.C. too, and when all the stationary devices had been disconnected, we were off.

My mother took my hand and Dad took command, wheeling me out of my room and past the nurses' station toward the elevator. A few had gathered to watch us go, broad smiles full of excitement and pride.

Mom and Dad made conversation, pointing out the waiting area where they went to get snacks and make phone calls. I smiled and nodded, paying little attention and swallowing the lump of fear building ever bigger in my throat. I was not even certain of what I was afraid, but fear it was, tightening its grip across my chest. Mom pushed the button and when the doors pulled open, Dad guided me in and I faced the back wall with a pounding heart as we were lowered 9 levels to the ground floor. He joked about having put me in backwards, and that I should fire him as my driver but I could not laugh. I mustered a smile and he smiled back, solemn, but proud.

The mirrored box came to a stop with a soft thud and the doors slid open. I breathed deeply. Dad pulled me backward out of the elevator and leaned over to speak into my ear. "Are you ready?" he whispered. I nodded without looking at him. My heart was beating furiously now, my face flushed with heat. He pushed me forward and around the corner and immediately everything froze. I gazed in awe at the scene before me.

A set of glass doors at the end of the deserted hallway framed long rays of sunlight streaming through, pooling on the floor. The light was so white and bright it was all I could see. My heart swelled and my breath caught in my throat. Suddenly I remembered. I had seen this before. This is what it had looked like when I had stood at the gates of heaven and felt the outstretched arms of God.

And then I understood. I had wanted death. I had hoped for heaven. I had been ready to leave this earthly life, and I had been robbed of my chance to be free of it. I had seen the pearly gates and I had been turned away. I would not feel God's arms around me in the welcome embrace of eternal peace. Death and heaven were not coming, not yet. I would have to live.

Huge tears streamed down my face without a sound and splashed into my lap but I would not blink fearful that if I closed my eyes for even a moment the magic would be lost. I sat in the chair shaking and sobbing silently as it rolled forward. Dad touched my shoulder, as if he heard my thoughts, though I knew he couldn't possibly understand.

Pushing toward the light and through the doors, I felt the sun on my skin as though for the first time. At its touch, my whole body quaked with emotion and I was utterly overcome. The feeling of the warm light on my face was like a kiss from life itself. I wanted to melt into it. This was the way it had felt when heaven had welcomed me home. I cried for its sanctuary... and mourned my loss of it.

Outside, every sense was ablaze with recognition. My nose filled with the smell of late summer - cool and fresh - and the taste of it in my mouth made my heart beat with wild excitement. Every hair stood on end. Wet cheeks felt the touch of the breath of life. I was powerfully aware of the smell of dirt, and grass, and tree sap. I could feel the brink of autumn in the air and the last of the summer sun. I could hear the trees whispering, their leaves shaking in the soft breeze, as though they were quaking with excitement to see me, welcoming me back.

I couldn't stop gasping for breath, savoring the cool air in my mouth and on my tongue. I watched my hand reach out to the shrub next to me, giggling through my tears at its touch. The leaves were stiff and waxy, and the sensation of them on my fingers sent me into another fit of laughter and tears. I could feel. More than just pain, I could feel joy.

I was alive. And I was glad.

TEN

Spring was threatening, the sun lingering longer in the sky, and the buds on the trees and bushes smelled of new life. It was late morning when I hobbled toward the large glass doors. A service technician was circling the building astride a Sportster, leaning his head toward his knees listening for an apparent knock that likely landed the bike there in the first place.

My heart fluttered. I was nervous.

A surprising number of new staff were moving about the floor. I was a stranger to them and that was a strange feeling. The narrow set of stairs to my office made me smile, and then immediately grimace.

Jensen and the rest of the staff greeted me enthusiastically, clearly avoiding conversation about the accident or my legs. I was glad, and grateful they ignored my dragging left leg and limp left arm. It felt good to see them again, it felt good to be working. It was different, somehow, and I had expected that. But it was good to be back. I cleaned off my desk and organized it, answered stacks of messages and emails, and stood to give hugs to periodic visitors. It was nice.

When Rusty came to see if I wanted lunch I could see the emotion in his eyes.

"How you feelin' kid?"

"Good. Pretty good."

"They said they'd move your office downstairs to the accounting department for awhile..."

"Yeah, I know. But the stairs are good for me. It'll only be hard for a little while. And I like being up here with everybody."

He nodded.

"The wife made you a quilt. I got it in the truck, if you want..." I smiled.

"Thank you! Tell her that means a lot."

He nodded again, shoving his hands in his pockets.

"Free for lunch today?"

"No, I can't. I'm only here for a few hours. I have physical therapy at 2."

"Bet that hurts."

I smiled, but I was already tired and I knew it showed.

"It doesn't feel good."

I had hoped he would laugh. I tried to.

He rocked his weight from one foot to the other and smoothed his beard.

"All right kid, well, maybe we can have lunch when you're done with physical therapy. You have a couple more weeks, or...?"

"Two more months." I grinned at the flash of surprise in his eyes. "But we can still have lunch sometime. We just have to go early. And maybe somewhere on the south side of town."

He nodded and I stood to hug him. I could see his steel eyes mist as I limped around my desk carrying my left arm which was showing improvement, but still lifeless from the elbow down.

"Good to have you back, kid. For awhile there we were pretty sure you weren't gonna make it." He pulled away from me and smiled quickly before he turned and took hold of the railing. "Careful down these stairs when you go," he said without looking back.

I nodded at his back. I could see it was bothering him again, watching him negotiate the narrow stairs, and my heart softened. I wasn't sure why this 65 year old bike mechanic and racing legend took such a liking to me, but he was like a grandfather now. He had visited me every day while I was in the hospital - even before I'd come out of the coma. When my mother had suggested he didn't need to be there he'd told her "You don't have to like me, you don't even have to talk to me. But I'm going to be here. Every day. So you might as well get used to it." She was alarmed and irritated initially, but he'd grown on her and now I was sure she thought the world of him. He loved me as if I were his own, and it didn't matter why.

By the time I left the building, my legs felt like columns of concrete and my knees were throbbing. Physical therapy was especially excruciating, but I had expected that too. There was pride in my heart when I pulled into the parking lot of my apartment building, but mostly, there was exhaustion. Getting out of my car took almost all my remaining strength and when I dropped myself on the concrete stoop I wondered for a second if I would be able to stand back up and make it up the stairs to my apartment.

Thumping the pack against my hand, I pulled a smoke out with my mouth. I hated that I was doing it, but it was comfortable and familiar, and I wanted those things the most. Today had been good. It had. But it hadn't been what I had thought. Forcing the first drag out between pursed lips I felt that same vacancy, that same exhaustion, that same diamond shaped yellow sign. I felt at home with the people - they were like family... but the work itself; the projects, the planning... didn't make me happy. Not like it once had. Even the thought of putting together the first vendor lists for the Rally didn't excite me. Even after all the dealership had done - cards, fundraisers, even setting up a computer in my room in the hospital so I could see the smiling faces of the people who had come to support me - I felt removed from it - from them somehow. My title and coworkers couldn't fill me like they once had. I was empty and unsettled again. Worse than before, and now I felt a sense of urgency I could not explain to make a decision, make a move toward a meaningful future.

I had been so excited to be able to walk again, move back into my apartment and get back to my job... I thought that returning to my life would fill me with a renewed sense of joy. I thought I would feel like I did those first few years at the dealership – rescued, somehow, hopeful and really happy. I didn't feel like that at all. I felt old, and weak... utterly unfulfilled, and running out of time.

I watched the smoke drift skyward in front of me and thought about Marianne, and her vision, and wondered what I could possibly have seen or heard that would make me want to live through this. There had to be something I was supposed to do... something that would make it all worth it, and bring me peace and happiness in the process. I was tired of just surviving, just getting through. I wanted joy. I wanted to LIVE, and I wanted to love it. But when I released my imagination to the possibilities the space was vacant and I was left with a desire for change and no idea where to begin. I knew if I could just find the right job in the right place, joy and I would meet like lost lovers and I would find myself in a new career, in a new city, and everything else would fall into place. I would love life, and find a partner to love it with me.

The butt of the smoke was hot between my fingers when I took the last drag and extinguished it against the concrete. How would I find it - the thing I'd been 'sent back' to do? I could think of no place, no job, no field of study that sparked passion - or even a glimmer of excitement in me.

The Rally was coming... *Maybe this time it will really happen,* I thought wistfully. Maybe this year it would finally bring me the new start I yearned for. Maybe some person among the throngs would unintentionally give me the direction and meaning and joy I had sought for so long. It was a weak hope, and a long shot, but it was all I had. Discouragement and frustration were pushing heavily against me.

I stood with a sigh and flicked the speckled yellow and brown filter into the sidewalk trashcan across from me. The buttons on the security pad clicked in their familiar pattern and I threw all my weight against the door to heave it open. The stairs in front of me were daunting, but home was waiting. I draped my limp arm onto the handrail and began the climb.

The Me I Was

***

"Why don't you finish your degree?" my mother asked as we made laps around their neighborhood one morning. "You're so close to finishing."

The full heat of summer was still a couple of weeks away but the morning was already warm and bright. I nodded, feeling neither one way or the other about it. For blocks I had regaled her with my desire to find the thing or place that would be my cornerstone, the thing that would give me a place to start.

I watched as the sun peeked over the crest of the hill in front of us, a tiny bit brighter each step until it bathed my face in its warmth. I closed my eyes for a moment and smiled to myself.

"... and it really just lays a good foundation for your future. I know you want..." She talked on about my future and the more I thought about it, the better it sounded. I had enjoyed college – my time in Laramie was among my fondest memories. I liked school and loved college life. Not Laramie though, not this time. It was time for something new, somewhere bigger, better.

I had always loved Colorado, despite my quick exit out of Denver - especially Boulder and Fort Collins. I loved the scenery, the culture, the shopping. I loved the sense of adventure, the healthy, active lives I imagined the people there lived. Maybe Colorado State would be my new place. I could be a Coloradoan. I liked the thought. I could be one of those stunning women who floats through life in a gauzy white skirt with bangles on her arm and bells on her ankles, eyes full of mystery and brilliance and the light of a joyful heart. I could be a great student, an avid outdoors woman and environmentalist. I could ride my bike to class and eat organic. I could be beautiful and magic and loved. I felt excitement tingle in me for the first time in a long time. Maybe this was what I had been waiting for. If destiny didn't knock on my door during the rally, I'd hunt her down in the mountains of the colorful State.

Summer was fully upon us when I got the fat envelope in the mail and signed up for Fall Semester classes. I made a couple quick trips to look for apartments and while the one in my dreams was not there, I found a suitable alternative and put down a deposit. I was a little apprehensive and a little excited. I had something to work toward. Soon I'd be in a new place starting my new life.

I told Jensen I would work through the Rally and then I would be going back to school. He was fully supportive. When one of the vendors heard about my plan, he offered to throw my bike in the back of his trailer after the show and haul it down there for me after the event – he had another one to do in Denver anyway. I hadn't ridden it since the accident, but I gratefully accepted his offer. The tingle that had come into my left arm several months ago had slowly - almost imperceptibly - spread to full use, and I knew I would be able to ride. I wanted to, someday. I was pretty sure I did, anyway.

Everything was falling into place. It was clear; Colorado State was going to be my new home. I would not be loading trailers or filing paperwork from an office on a big rig – I was going back to school. I would be taking classes and studying. I'd spend weekends hiking or biking or skiing. I'd just accidentally get into the best shape of my life and feel really beautiful for the first time. I'd take a yoga class and learn to cook really good, healthy food. Maybe my skin would finally be clear. I would make great friends and talk passionately about my version of God and politics and relationships. Maybe I'd even meet my partner and get started on happily ever after.

As the heat of summer grew to a swelter, I began to pack my little apartment. I was nervous, but I assured myself I would love it. I wrapped plates in newspaper and boxed up winter clothes, daydreaming about how wonderful my new life would be. I imagined riding my bicycle to the food co-op after class, laptop in my messenger bag slung across my back.

I'd make dinner to my favorite music and study while I ate. Maybe a friend would come over for a glass of wine later and we'd walk to the park. But no matter how deeply I immersed myself in the vision, I couldn't really feel it. The excitement was gone. It wasn't the packing. I loved packing. I liked moving even, mostly. It was something else. A fear of change, perhaps, carried over from the hospital?

I tried to ignore it as I immersed myself in my work, thankful for long hours and busy days to keep me from dwelling on it too long. When the nights were quiet, and I couldn't keep my mind from spinning, I'd remind myself why I should be excited, why it was good, but still the feeling persisted. Finally one evening a couple of days before the Rally, I called Marianne, fighting back tears.

"I don't get it," I told her, my chest tight. "I keep imagining myself there, walking to class with a cup of coffee and my laptop and I'm trying to feel how excited and happy I am. But I'm not. It's all grey and cloudy... I feel sad. What does it mean?"

"Don't worry too much about it, Jaci," she said gently. "Often people that have been through traumatic experiences get a little weird energy around the anniversary of the incident." I hadn't realized until she mentioned it - my moving date was almost a year to the day.

Understanding the feeling helped, and I immediately calmed down. It would be ok. I would be ok. It was the right thing to do, after all.

"Thank you, Marianne," I said as I hung up. "I appreciate you so much."

The Sturgis Rally was as hot, crazy, and exhausting as it always was... and this year I liked it less. A good sign in my mind. Every year I got a little better at it though and by this, my third year helping to manage the chaos, I had time to meet a friend and co-worker for lunch at the concession area.

"I feel like crap" I told her when I sat down.

"It's only day two." She said dryly. "You realize that."

I grinned weakly at her humor. "Yeah, I know. It's

weird though. My shoulders and neck are super tight and I'm exhausted."

"Of course they are, of course you are. It's the freakin' Sturgis Rally. At Black Hills Harley-Davidson®. And you run your ass off out here." I laughed at her again and watched her cut through a corn dog with her teeth, just missing the stick.

"Oh, it's not that bad," I protested, forcing a smile. "I don't have nearly as much to do as the first year out here. That, was crazy." She grinned and swallowed, then gave me her best 'skeptical mom' eyes.

"You go out last night?"

"No!" I asserted. "That's what's so weird. I went to bed early. SUPER early. And the night before too."

She looked at me sideways, this time with genuine concern. "You never get sick." She furrowed her brow. "I think you should go to the free clinic. Just see what's going on."

"Naw. It can't be that big a deal. I probably just got a weird flu-ish thing going on." She shrugged.

"Suit yourself. I'm going to the Aerosmith concert at the campground tonight with Seth." I grinned knowingly.

"So... you'll be in late tomorrow?"

"Pffttthhh," she scoffed. "I won't be in at ALL tomorrow."

I looked at her in mock admiration of her sass.

"It's my day off," she confessed with a grin and threw her corndog stick into the giant trashcan at the end of the table. "What about you?"

"Oh, I'm definitely just going to bed tonight." There was worry in her eyes when she held my gaze.

"You really do feel like shit don't you? Well, call me if you need anything. Seriously. Aerosmith or not. Seth or not. I can come over." I shook my head.

"No, no... I will not be bothering you for any reason. I love you, and I appreciate your concern, but even if there was something wrong, there are plenty of people I can call who are not at a live concert of their favorite band with the man of their dreams." She faked shy and giggled like a 16 year old girl.

"Well, if you insist..." I grinned and hugged her before I headed back to my golf cart. *Only 7 more hours* I thought as I turned the key and took off across the lot.

True to my word, I went home after work and immediately to sleep. I was sick all night and thought it was just the vendor food but as the early hours of daylight came rushing, it only got worse. I was so thirsty I couldn't sleep but as soon as I took a drink it came right back up. I begrudgingly called Jensen and spent the day on the couch. And the next day too. Two days later I willed it to be over. My stomach muscles ached from heaving and I was exhausted beyond my prior understanding of the word. The last weekend of the rally had come as I drifted in and out of sleep. I'd have missed it all together if my mother hadn't come to help pack my apartment. When she saw me she demanded I go to the hospital. I watched the last of the bikes streaming out of town from her passenger window as she rushed me to the ER. I had contracted the West Nile virus and meningitis.

***

September leaves stirred beneath the little bistro table where I sat, the unnatural bluish light beaming from the blank, virtual page. I watched the sky blush with dusk, lit a cigarette and gazed down the street at the flashing streetlight. In a moment of inspiration I balanced my smoke on the table's edge and let my fingers fly wildly over the keys before I had nothing more to say and sat back again, brooding over my thoughts and their translation to the page.

I loved nights like these when I could be anonymous, unnoticed, and lose myself in the wanderings of my mind. Main street was warm, and quiet, save for scatters of people shuffling by and the constant drone of traffic. The store front light that shown down on me from above, was neither bothersome nor useful – just there. The wheezing of a harmonica stretched across the dark streets and I strained to hear its tune. Here and there the low rumble of a motorcycle would filter into my focused thoughts and the sound of it gave me pause. I missed it. I really did.

My doctor had informed me that under stress, meningitis can spread to the brain and cause paralysis or even death. He had advised against moving and starting school. I had backed out of my lease, cancelled my enrollment and made arrangements for my motorcycle to be held until I could come pick it up.

I should have trusted myself, I thought. My whole body cringed when I thought about the huge chunk of money I had lost because of it. An expensive lesson. The financial setback was tough, but it wasn't the worst part. The last two words in the paragraph before me encompassed the most painful part of the whole experience; what now? I had still been in the hospital after my last day at the Harley shop had come and gone, and I spent the next few weeks recuperating. I didn't consider going back - my heart really didn't want to anyway. This was the third year I had been in the hospital during or just after the rally, the third year I had missed my birthday, the third year I spent all the money I had earned working overtime on medical bills, and spent the last weeks of summer completely incapacitated. I took it as a sign.

Another long drag and I balanced the last inch of the smoke on the edge of the green metal table, and resumed typing. The words that strung across the page were not angry... just sad. I rambled on in page after page dreaming of the same things I had been seeking for the last several years - hell, all of my adult life; a definition for myself, a place where I belonged - where I mattered. If I could find that, I would find happy. I was irritated by my presence here at all, and my heart ached when I remembered where I had been and what it had felt like before I woke up in the ICU last year. There had been no white light, no pearly gates, but that peaceful joy, the incredible lightness and warmth was permanently impressed on me, on the memory of my very soul. What the hell was I supposed to do here that was worth leaving that for?

I took a final drag and put out the smoke, pressed the screen against the keyboard and, tucking the thing under my arm, headed for home. The voice of the lonely harmonica followed me and I heard the last strains of its tune as I mounted the stairs to my apartment, letting the heavy door swing shut on the music of the street.

Jaclyn Lanae

The Me I Was

ELEVEN

The sun was almost red, blinking through the trees on the eastern horizon as we headed out of town. Dad had a conference in Memphis and tickets out of Denver were cheap. When Mom asked if I would give them a ride to the city, I secretly hoped maybe it was an answer to my burning questions. Maybe I was being guided "home". School wasn't "it", but maybe Colorado was. Anyway, I didn't have a job so I welcomed the opportunity, and took a little vacation of my own.

The entirety of the six-hour trip I dreamed of the possibility that I would find it there. My sign. My ticket. My key. Maybe I would run across an ad for an Event Planner or Promoter and land a job. Or someone would chat me up in a coffee shop downtown and refer me to my dream career. Or I'd meet my Mister and our lives together would set me to my life's work. I'd pick my parents up from the airport a week later and announce that I had found a place to live and I would not be going back with them. *I just hadn't been ready before*, I thought. I had rushed into it and now that I had lived through what I had, it was time. Maybe this was finally it.

I dropped them off at the airport and passed the ensuing days wandering the shops downtown, leafing through magazines and newspapers, touring the city. I found a favorite bookstore and spent hours at the bistro tables outside their doors reading, writing or just watching the people go by. I browsed boutiques I couldn't afford to shop in, and ate appetizers for meals at restaurants I had heard about in rave reviews. I drank too much coffee and spent whole afternoons on park benches. It would have been lovely, if it weren't so sad.

There was no ad, no job, no magic interaction. There was no clear path. Denver wasn't it. I had been wrong. I got lost almost everywhere I went, even in the areas I remembered well. I felt unsettled, and unhappy and it was not the way I had expected to feel. I had thought it would be like coming home.

On my last night in the city I sat on the hotel bed, waiting for the morning flight that would bring my parents home, flipping through hundreds of channels before I finally turned the TV off. For a long while I listened to the sounds of traffic on I-25 and let my mind wander. There weren't many places for it to go... I couldn't even dream about what I wanted because I had no idea what it was. It was not long before it wandered to the trip home and the emptiness that awaited me. My heart beat was heavy and I felt desperation squeezing my chest. I was all out of ideas. Then tears were streaming down my face and I felt my heart breaking. I just wanted it to be over - again. I was tired of searching, tired of struggling, tired of hurting, tired of healing, tired of hoping. All I wanted was direction and all I got was silence. Roadblocks. Dead-ends.

My heart ached. If this was the way life was going to be... then at least I wanted love. Deep passionate love. I gasped and sobbed with renewed vigor at the realization; not only was I lost... I was lonely. The truth and weight of my emotions settled heavily on me and I let the tears stream. *I'm ready*, I begged a higher power I wouldn't define, almost without realizing it. *Please. Bring me the man that understands me.*

I had cried all I could and when my breath returned to normal, I let my puffy eyes blink open. Night was heavy on the mountains outside my window. I felt a little better. More empty of the sad, at least. I took a bath and studied my misshapen legs and jagged, angry scars. I sighed and pushed the self-pitying thought out of my mind before it had even fully formed. There was nothing that could be done about it anyway. I leafed idly through Eco Home magazines while the water cooled to tepid, got out and dried myself before slipping under the covers, and fell asleep with my hair wet and the TV on.

The Me I Was

I spent the next morning in a much better mood, wandering the aisles of a little bookstore near the hotel with a French cookie and a very tall paper cup, steam curling through the sipping hole. Every inch was crammed with titles; some new, some thoroughly read, in not-so-orderly rows or stacked in the spaces between the tops of the books and the bottom of the shelves above. I wandered down each aisle, absently nibbling on my breakfast and browsing the deep shelves with my head cocked sideways to read the spines. Among them, a modest paperback that caught my eye with a bright cover and two lovely scripted words: New York. My heart fluttered. I had harbored grand dreams of a life in that city for some years and it occurred to me that it might just be the move I needed. I could sell my car, find an apartment and a job, and live the life I dreamed of my freshman year of college. I had grown, I reasoned, I was a different woman. Maybe now was the time. And I hadn't actually gone before. I had headed for a city – Denver - but what I had really wanted was THE city. I had wanted New York.

I landed in the driver's seat of my father's car with half a Peppermint Mocha and Newcomer's Guide to New York shoved deep into my purse, and headed for the airport. I didn't even take the book out of my bag on the ride home, certain I was successfully avoiding a heated discussion about the wisdom of such a decision. Mom and Dad chatted about their trip, the incredible shops and restaurants... and I listened, imagining tales of my own, my new life in the Big Apple. I would find a job and live in a little studio apartment. I'd walk everywhere and spend my time off in parks and bookstores and museums. I'd eat really good food and attend chic house parties. I'd go to plays and independent movies and travel the east coast. Every possibility was in New York. I might share a cab with an author or PR mogul or film executive. Surely I would find the person I was supposed to be in one of the greatest cities of the world. It wouldn't matter what else I did because I'd be from New York.

Back home I immediately devoured the guide and wandered around online listings looking up apartments and jobs. I told no one of my plan, sure they would only discourage me. I was excited. And a little nervous. So I called Darla.

We had met years ago, when we both worked in the chiropractor's office, and she had been as important in my life as Marianne. A massage therapist and powerful intuitive, when I was questioning everything in my life – my marriage most of all - I had laid on her table and felt such a sense of peace, comfort and hope in her readings.

She told me she had discovered the gift when she was practicing massage on a friend and felt compelled to share the thoughts and images coming to her. They hadn't seen each other in years when Darla ran into her friend one day and was bewildered by the woman's passionate expressions of gratitude. When Darla asked what she was thanking her for, the woman reminded Darla about their session, and told her that the messages Darla had shared with her had dramatically changed her life for the better. She had done some of the things she had always wanted to do and had never had the courage to follow through with.

The same had been true for me. I never much heard clear instructions like 'go here' or 'do that', just messages of hope and assurance. That I was on the right path, that I needed to open my heart and trust myself, and so on. I always left her sessions feeling rejuvenated in body and spirit. As I planned to move to one of the biggest cities on earth, I reached out to her again.

I didn't tell her my plan - not at first. I just wanted to see what she had to say. Truthfully, I was hoping I might get some insight, some confirmation I was doing the right thing. I'd tell her afterward, and then I'd tell her goodbye.

Her voice was soft above me, and I heard good things, loving things. I was reminded that I needed to be fearless and see myself living the life I wanted. I grinned inwardly. *Maybe the life I want is just a week and a three-hour flight away.* I thought about New York and tried to see myself living there, full of joy and success in every area of my life when Darla's voice stopped mid sentence and said "New York is not the place for you right now".

My skin pimpled, hairs standing on end and tears welled in my eyes. There was no way she could have known that had been my plan. I only half listened as she finished the reading and throughout the massage I continued to come back to the same question; what now? After the massage I told her of my plan and we marveled at the power and magic of what I called the Universe. I asked her if she had seen any clear paths for me and she simply shook her head. I thanked her kindly for her help and support and left her studio feeling peaceful… and more lost than ever.

Jaclyn Lanae

TWELVE

The trees had entirely pushed off their fiery leaves when I found myself standing in the season pass line for Terry Peak. The rental shop smelled just like I remembered - like sweaty boots, wet wool, and warm wax. The kids in front of me wore jeans that stuck tightly to their ankles and hoodies that hung past their pants pockets. Or Halloween costumes – it was the last day of October and the last day of the half-price season pass sale. "Yeah, man," the teenager in front of me was saying as we shuffled forward, "they told me I had to get pass insurance this year. I only got three days in last year before I hit that sick new pipe and busted my arm. Dad was pissed." My knees ached already - just from standing in line - and my stomach twisted. Something fluttered in my chest. I was nervous. And embarrassed by it. I forced thoughts of surrender out of my mind, took deep, calming breaths that I hoped were interpreted as boredom, and tried to remind myself I could do this.

I had practically been born in ski boots - my grandfather was a part of the group that brought the first real ski area to the Black Hills. He'd even carried some of the original posts up the side of the mountain for the first poma lifts. He was devoted to the sport and spent every weekend on the mountain. Consequently, my father and his siblings did too. My dad had been an incredible talent and despite his modest training grounds, went on to win gold in the downhill category at the 1974 National Collegiate Athletic Association competition and was named a First Team All American. At one time, my father had been the fastest (and most talented, as far as I was concerned) downhill skier in the country. He was slated for the Olympics but his sport had been dropped - it was too fast and too dangerous. He skied professionally for a couple of years before he decided to marry my Mom and find a more lucrative career to support the family he hoped to raise. I was just over two years old when they stuffed Kleenex in the smallest pair of rental boots Terry Peak had and sent me down the hill for the first time.

I didn't remember learning how to ski – it seemed like I had just always known. And I had always loved it. Even while I was in Laramie 'broke' couldn't keep me from it. I hitched rides to the mountains of Colorado whenever I could and stayed in hostels with friends-of-friends. I wasn't incredibly good at it or anything, I certainly didn't have my father's talent, but I loved it. I loved the ebb and flow of my body, driving forward and hard into the turn and then floating lightly across the glistening surface. I loved the wind tugging at my ponytail and the sting of blood pulsing in my thighs. I loved the exhilaration and exhaustion, breathing hard in the lift lines after a great run. I thought it was possibly the best form of exercise; you workout on the way *down* the hill... and you rest on the way *up*.

Last year I had just been released from the rehab hospital when the season began and it had not even been a consideration. It had also been one of the only seasons I had ever missed. This year I'd do something I loved again. This year, I would ski. When it was my turn in line, I signed a tiny receipt for a big chunk of money and went home to try on my boots.

Just walking across the carpeted living room of my apartment was uncomfortable. Above and beyond the general discomfort of hard plastic ski boots. This was different. Scary. The weight of them on my knees brought to mind images of the single remaining tendon in my right knee snapping, and the bottom half of my legs just falling off half-way up the lift. Or pulling my newly re-built left knee apart at the seams where it had been stitched back together. But I had a custom-made brace for each knee, courtesy of my stellar insurance, and I'd been assured after months of physical therapy that it was safe, as long as I was careful – this was not the time to pursue a career in freestyle aerial half-pipe riding. I had laughed out loud at the idea. Even before the accident, I would never have pursued such a thing, but now... Now even walking was scary.

The accident had given me a lot of things; a great story, a plethora of scars, a chance to take the elevator for a month and not feel bad about it. I think the External Fixators are still in a box in my father's garage. But I hadn't expected the fear. Loads and loads of fear. The fear that I would fall and my body would literally come apart at all the little pink seams was always with me. Every crack in the sidewalk was a potential catastrophe, every curb a small cliff. My body didn't work like it used to. And I was afraid like I never had been before. Of everything. For the last year, everything had hurt; every touch, every motion... I didn't trust my body, and my body didn't trust me. Still... I had loved skiing, the way it felt, and I wanted to feel that good again.

I knew it wouldn't be easy. I knew I wouldn't just show up, click into my skis, and take on the double black diamonds again. As it was, I could barely manage my half-hour walk up and down the boulevard every night. I needed to build more strength, a lot more, and walking alone wasn't going to do it. I needed to sweat, to pant. My knees couldn't take running which was fine with me – I had never much liked it anyway. And I hated the gym... so I got myself a bike. It was the ideal form of exercise for a body with a lot of broken parts and my inner environmentalist was rejoicing. It was perfect.

Only it wasn't.

I awkwardly wrestled my new KONA from the backseat of my car after some struggle and got the front tire back on. The afternoon was unusually warm and I thought how nice my walk would be as I carried my bike upstairs. It was silly, I knew, but I wanted to wait, just a little while. I needed to ask someone to be sure it was set up right; that I'd gotten the seat on at the right height, and that the brakes were adjusted and working properly. I walked the next night too. Maybe I should plan my route. And I probably shouldn't go alone the first time... By the third night, I felt like a complete failure. *Geezus Jaci*, I thought as I sat and stared at the thing leaning in the corner of my bedroom. *What made you think you could do this? How the hell are you going to ski if you can't even get on a bike?* I stared at it for a minute longer, admiring the fresh silver paint and the simple lines. I could take it back tomorrow. *It's sure pretty... makes for an expensive art piece though.* But as soon as I surrendered to my new plan, I knew how I would feel. Like a failure. Like a scared, lazy, hollow shell of a person just waiting to die. *Damn it, no. This is not who I wanted to be. I know how to ride a bicycle. I just need to get on the damn thing and do it.* I'd start with a short ride, I rationalized. Just to the top of the boulevard and back.

I wheeled my shiny new beast down the hallway and to the top of the stairs. Now what? There was no way my knees could take the extra weight *and* lower me safely from one stair to the other. Hell, I didn't even trust them to do that when it was just the weight of my body and my shoes. The handrail was on my right, and I knew I'd need it to steady myself... so I clutched the top of the forks just below the handlebars with the little strength that had returned to my left arm, and let the front tire tip over the edge of the top stair as slowly as possible. It was mostly a controlled fall from there; my feet moved faster than they had in months to stay ahead of the descending bike and I grasped at the hand railing, holding us both back and then releasing to catch up with the fall only to grasp ahold of it again before my bike and I spilled through the door and onto the stoop.

Now there was a little victory dance mixed with the fear churning through my veins. I took a deep breath, steadied myself, and swung my leg over the bar. I shifted my weight too quickly though, and almost went right on over it before I did a couple quick little hops and landed with both feet solidly astraddle. Another deep breath. By the time I shifted my weight back onto my right leg and pulled the other up far enough to rest it on the pedal I was nervous. Really nervous. Just having my knee bent at that angle was painful. What was I doing? Maybe it wasn't a good idea to go alone. I had already crashed a time or two just walking! It really probably wasn't safe. Or a good idea. I could just go for a walk later. Design TV was on. And I had hot chocolate. The idea was appealing for only a split second. *No. No!* I didn't want to be that woman, that person. I could do this. I wanted it. I needed it.

I took a deep breath and pushed myself up and back... and jammed my tailbone into the nose of my seat before my feet kicked off the pedals and both landed on the ground, hard. My heart pounded, and my fearful, couch potato self whined loudly. *See? That really hurt. And it could have been so much worse. Thank God it has an angled downtube.* I forced a little laugh, and tried again, this time successfully landing squarely on the seat. I took a few wobbly strokes and then I was off. The first crosswalks were wildly intimidating and I loathed coming to a complete stop only to have to build up all my momentum again. But, it was better than being run over and there were only a few of them before the streets turned entirely residential. Then I could – largely – ride right down the middle of the street without coming across a single car.

The naked trees looked eerily beautiful against the blushing sky and I felt excitement, joy and pride blow past my face as the wind tangled my hair. I was a little surprised. I had forgotten how good it felt to breathe hard, and really push my muscles. It felt good to be doing something good for myself. *I'm so glad I did this!* The thought had no more fully formed before fear crept up behind it in my mind. *You're going too fast! Slow down! What if a pebble makes your tire jump? What if you skid out on the gravel in the road?* I panicked and grabbed the brakes hard, slowing way down. Then chastised myself. I couldn't have been going more than 5 or 10 miles per hour. And there was no way I would "skid out". Even before the accident, when I had trained with my father and we had ridden as hard and fast as possible, I had never "skidded out". Except that one time when I didn't hear his instruction to turn and we t-boned at 35 miles an hour. But that was purely accidental, and circumstantial, I rationalized; it had nothing to do with going too fast. I remembered laughing at the memory... and now it made me cringe. *You never know what could happen.* I felt as though I were scolding myself, and yet dutifully turned around.

Fear and I fought all the way home, and on every trip thereafter. It was such a strong presence in my mind, I manifested it all over my fair city. I repeatedly found myself lying in a twisted heap beneath my bike and backpack when the light turned green at the busiest intersections in town. I could almost hear the collective gasps of horror from inside the idling vehicles.

I didn't get it. I had ridden bikes rather successfully on and off most of my life. Oh sure, I had the usual gory knee-scrape and pedal-down-the-shin incidents... but I could ride. You wouldn't have known it now. No matter how small the threat - every crack in the sidewalk, every tiny rock - was a disaster waiting to happen. That black tar they use to seal cracks in the road was the scariest of all. Sticky when warm, I was certain I'd be pedaling along and get my front tire in it, and then before I knew it I'd be lying on my back in the middle of the street.

I wanted to want to ride my bike. I thought it would get easier with practice – and it did, to some degree - but certainly not enough. I fell at least once or twice a week and even though there was never much for damage, my pride and confidence were nearly shot. I was losing patience, and any interest I had in figuring out how to make it work.

I knew it wasn't just my compromised body. Sure, I had a warped sense of balance, my knees didn't flex all the way, my ankle had been put back on a little crooked – but it was more than that. I was afraid. Not just afraid, terrified. And that maybe bothered me more than the struggle itself. I had not forgotten how to ride a bike. I had forgotten how not to be terrified.

THIRTEEN

I could tell from the way the worry lines in the corners of his eyes deepened that he was nervous. It wasn't about the skiing. My father and I were close enough that I knew that much for sure. He was calm, certain, as he always was. I'm sure he thought that if - worst case scenario - I had lost all ability, he would start from the beginning and teach me again, just like he had for hundreds of children and adults throughout his skiing career. The easy conversation and laughter that was our usual lapsed and we fell silent even before we were fully out of town. He was nervous, I was sure, because I was.

The braces for my knees sat in a bag between us, shiny and new, and a little daunting. I sipped my coffee and glanced at the clock. 7:45. We'd be on the mountain in an hour. One hour.

I watched as the snow laden trees rolled past us on the interstate and wondered for a moment if he hadn't taken the other way because it would have taken us past Falling Rock. I liked that way better. It was prettier. We'd always gone that way, when I was a kid. It was faster, Dad said, but later in life I learned that was only because he pushed the limits of "legal" when it came to speed. I had never been afraid though. My father had been driving those roads all of his life. He knew them like the back of his hand. He was not reckless, he was practiced.

"Is your coffee good?"

"Yeah, really good. Thank you". I smiled at the side of his face, hoping to convey the love and appreciation I had for him, and his patience with me. I wanted to tell him that I was scared, that I wanted to go back, but I was too embarrassed to admit my fear in front of him so I stared out the window.

"I love the snow when it looks like this," he said, glancing quickly at me. "It just sparkles in the sunlight".

"Me too," I said, with as much emotion as I could convey, wishing I were a child again and I could curl up on his lap and let him tell me I had nothing to fear because he was here, and be able to believe it. The fact that he was here with me, and would be all day, was very comforting. But I knew now, in a way I had never known a person could understand, that even if he were with me for every step, even if he could literally hold my hand, he would never truly be able to take the danger away. No one could. More than that even, life in my body would always be different. I would have to try to avoid the accidents and slip ups that littered our lives in a body that just wasn't as capable of getting out of the way. That was a fact. Dad at my side or not, I could still fall. The lone ligament in my right knee could still tear. My legs and arms could still be broken - plates screwed into them or not. No one and nothing could really guarantee safety from anything, and I was more fragile than before. I would just have to be "careful".

"Need to stop at the Fill n' Go?"

I smiled and shook my head. "No, thanks." Then, "On second thought, yeah. I'd rather go to the bathroom here than up on the mountain." He laughed harder than he otherwise would have and I was sorry it was so forced between us now. When I slid out of the passenger seat and onto the hard packed snow of the parking lot I felt my knees ache in protest of the work. *I haven't even put boots on yet I thought glumly.*

He had a bag of my favorite kind of almonds when I got back in the truck and offered me some immediately. I took a few and a long chug of water, and we headed into the canyon for the last stretch of the trip. "Remember when you got your first driving lesson? In the old truck?" I grinned and nodded. "Couldn't get you to stop driving off the end of the hood. Down here in these turns you'd be going along fine and then just hit the brakes out of nowhere." He was laughing now, genuinely, and the sound was comforting.

110

The Me I Was

It was true. For the first year of my life as an automobile operator, I drove by staring at the end of the hood and watching where it met the center line. Which, of course, left me woefully unprepared for corners and I'd panic, adjusting my speed - dramatically - when I saw the yellow line turn sharply in front of me. It had been a series of jarring driving lessons for my father. *And for Jess*, I thought, softening at the memory of her sitting quietly in the passenger seat, a miserable and terrified look on her little face. Fifteen years later he still laughed at the memory and reminiscing had served well to distract me from the new fear I was about to face.

Every winter weekend since before I could remember we'd been coming to this mountain. After Grandpa died, we all kind of quit working there and just came up to ski or race. When there was no longer need to clock in at the main lodge - Stewart Lodge - on the "bunny hill" side of the mountain, we'd begun parking on the lower side, at the Nevada Gulch lodge, home of the locally infamous Dark Horse saloon. It had always been the "cooler" of the two lodges, defined as such, in part, by the necessity of skill to get there. It wasn't hard, *per se*... but there wasn't a beginner level slope to be found on this side of the mountain either. If you parked at the Nevada Gulch lodge, you had to at least kind of know what you were doing.

That side of the mountain boasted all the most difficult terrain, and the Dark Horse itself was a harbor of true ski culture. There was a fireplace inside the bar, old skis nailed to the walls and ceiling, and photos of my father and other legends of the mountain in cheap wooden frames. I hadn't been allowed in as a child under 21, but I had known it as the place where the cool, older kids went. When I was finally old enough, my father and I had enjoyed one of our first beers together at a table by the fireplace inside. My heart ached and I was washed with embarrassment as we passed the turnoff for Nevada Gulch and headed up the hill to Stewart. I was certain I could feel my father fumble around in his mind for something to say, but I excused him from it by staring out my window. I knew. He had done the right thing.

He carried my skis and stood in line to pay for his ticket, and I wrestled my boots and duffle up the wide stairs toward the main floor of the lodge. I couldn't believe what an effort it was to get to the top and when I finally stood there, nearly panting, taking in the familiar view of windows and tables from my childhood, I wondered if this were maybe the worst idea I had ever had. My pride saved me from tucking tail and asking my father to take me home, and instead he found me struggling to get my foot into my boots when he came up the stairs. The lodge was, thankfully, almost empty at this hour, so there were few to see the tears of pain and frustration welling up in my eyes. My slightly crooked ankle was fiercely resisting the flex and angle necessary to drive it into the boot and I was sure I could literally feel my femur twist against the plate and screws in my thigh. Getting the boots on had been hard at home, when they were warm and pliable. After days in Dad's garage – he'd taken them to adjust my bindings and tune my skis - and an hour in the backseat of his truck, they felt to me like concrete. I pushed through the pain and finally my heel landed on the foot bed and I sat down in relief, blinking away the tears as he approached.

"How's it going?"

"Good. Little harder getting into my boots than it used to be." I had wanted it to be funny but the residual frustration incited a look of compassion on my father's face as he patted my back.

"Anything I can do?"

"No, I'm fine. Oh! Um, actually, I would love a glass of water." He nodded and jumped up.

"I'll be right back."

I thought how oddly comfortable it was to have these terribly uncomfortable ski boots on while I dug through my duffel for the knee braces. If I hurried, I could have them on before he got back. I pulled down my ski pants and sat down in my long underwear, fitting the plastic hinged brace to my leg before wrapping the long straps of industrial strength Velcro around my thigh, above and below my knee. There was an order to the process, I knew, but I couldn't quite remember what my physical therapist had told me. As soon as I stood up, ready to pull up my snow pants I knew I'd done it wrong. It was too tight. I could see my Dad working his way back toward me, attempting to spill as little as possible from two plastic cups as he delicately clunked across the floor in his boots. I sat back down in surrender, loosened the straps, and began again. He was patient, chatting enthusiastically about the adventure before us as I repeated the process first on one leg, then on the other, stood to check the fit, and finally pulled up my pants. Coat, hat, goggles, gloves. The blood was already being squeezed from my right calf as we headed out to click into our skis. I was again surprised at how heavy my legs felt with the boots on and simultaneously proud of how well I was walking in them. For a moment it was as though nothing had happened, as though my body were as capable as it had been two years ago, and I smiled.

The crisp mountain air stung my cheeks and filled my lungs with frosty cold. I clipped into my skis without missing a beat and a moment later we were gliding down the trail toward the new high speed quad. I was glad my father thought I could bypass the very easiest runs and start with some blue squares, and was mid-thought, wondering how well I would actually do when the inside edge of my left ski caught and twisted away from me. Searing, white-hot pain shot up through my knee and into my thigh and I let out a squeal but he was too far in front of me to hear it. I kept my balance, pulled my wayward ski back and kept the braces over my knees tightly pressed together until I slid into the lift line.

"How'd it go?"

"Good. It was good. I'll just have to take it slow."

"Of course," he said, compassion in his face. "You're the boss today... wherever you want to go."

I want to go home. I was embarrassed by the thought. "Let's just make a few runs here on Yellow," I replied, referring to the lift we were on.

I had always liked the run right under the chair. Long and wide, it made for great giant slalom type turns, which were my favorite. The bottom of the run finished with The Falls, an exhilaratingly short, steep drop that had been taken out years ago when the new lift was put in. I assumed it was an effort to make the high speed quad and it's associated runs more accessible to a mid-level skier. Those of us who had loved the mountain and grown up on its slopes though, were sad to see it go. Today however, I was grateful my run would end easily at the top of The Falls where the line for the new lift started.

I stared straight ahead, watching familiar trees and trail markers go by below while my father chatted with the stranger that had boarded the chair with us. The sun was bright, reflecting off the snow and when I glanced at my dad his face was bathed in its gold hue. The calm that settled over me with the familiar sights and sounds was nervous, and when the final tower on the crest of the last ridge of the mountain came into view all "calm" was gone. I knew how to exit a ski lift chair. I had done it thousands of times. At LEAST thousands. That consolation did almost nothing to soothe my nerves as our chair made steady progress to the top. What if I caught a tip and was drug under the chair? What if my binding released and I stepped out of my ski? What if this stranger cut me off and I fell over him? I had my poles out several minutes before it was necessary, every muscle of my body tensed in anticipation of what was apparently going to be the hardest thing I had ever done. I was sure my father wondered at my novice actions, but he politely said nothing. Finally, the chair slowed dramatically, making it possible to simply stand up and be pushed forward until the chair made its turn and started the decent. Somewhere between hauling myself to standing and getting my poles out in front of me, though, I panicked. The chair was taking too long to nudge the back of my thighs. I was too far forward. Or was I too far back? I began to twist around to orient myself when I finally got the nudge I'd been waiting for and lurched forward, leaving one of my poles stuck in the snow. I fell forward and down - almost in slow motion -

landing in a little heap of legs and skis directly in the path of exiting skiers. I struggled to get up, washed in embarrassment as the teenage lift-op smashed the red emergency stop button and ran out to clear the path of the debris that was me. My father made a couple quick side hops up the rise to retrieve my abandoned pole and was back at my side helping me up before I fully understood what had happened. He gently ushered me out of the way and the Lifty re-started the chair. I dusted myself off and looked miserably at my father. He pulled my hat off and slapped it across his muscled thigh a few times to shake the snow free, and handed it back to me with a smile. He gazed out at the vista from the top of the mountain while I re-organized myself and when he saw that I was dressed and buckled, patted me on the back.

"Ready?" I nodded, unconvinced I would ever really be "ready". He gestured for me to lead and I shook my head.

"You go first. It's easier for me if I can focus on you."

He nodded in acceptance and started down the slope. I took a deep breath and let my skis tip forward, shifting my weight ever so slightly to the front of the long boards stretched out before me, letting gravity pull me slowly down the top section of the mountain. *What am I doing?!* I thought to myself as I began to pick up speed. My feet were already killing me, every muscle in my body was as tight as a drum, and I hadn't even been able to get off the lift. Worse yet, I was snowplowing down the run as if it were my first day on skis. The posture hurt my knees badly, but I wasn't about to pull my feet together and turn properly, I was already going too fast. Far too fast. I was terrified. And this was the easy run.

Midway down the pain in my knees was just too much to continue to snowplow, so I took to making a turn or two correctly, and stopping. Making another turn or two and stopping again. I was horrified, both at what I thought was the way I must have looked from the chair above, and at my own sudden ineptitude on skis. At each stop I looked down the run at the hard-packed corduroy that had always been my playground, and now saw nothing but impending devastation;

hundreds of little piles of snow that lay in wait to catch an edge and twist my knee right out of its socket. By the time we stood in line the second time, my feet were almost numb and my thighs were throbbing. Again, I was sure I could feel the muscle in my leg working against the titanium plate.

Oh my god, what have I done? I thought. I unbuckled my boots for the ride back up the lift and gave a little sigh of relief as blood rushed back into my feet and ankles. It was a trick I had learned from my father back in my racing days. Super stiff boots made for great control, but were not kind to calves that were - in his case - over muscled, and in my case, just too close to my ankles, a situation complicated by the fact that chunks of my leg were missing and, when the skin grafts had stuck to the bone as they healed, the muscle had bunched up even farther below the knee. By the time we were moving back up the mountain, I was sure both my legs would drop to the snow beneath me. I was miserable.

"How was it?" I nodded awkwardly.

"I'd forgotten how uncomfortable ski boots are the first few days of the season," I told him, trying to laugh.

He grinned. "Yeah, they aren't really designed for comfort are they?" I smiled back. "You looked a little stiff there, at first," he said gently. I knew he was being kind. He must have been mortified... him, a legend on the mountain and his daughter, a fumbling, incompetent mess.

"I just keep feeling like I'm going too fast, so I keep stopping," I confessed. "It's like I need a slow wax." He laughed, but not the way I had hoped, and patted my knee.

"Just turn more. Eventually, it'll be just like riding a bike." I knew he meant it to be re-assuring.

I was never more grateful to get out of my boots and into the car as I was at the end of a couple hours that day. I was as embarrassed in front of myself as I was in front of him. Why couldn't I do this? It had been a year since I graduated from rehab and moved back into my own apartment. I should be over it by now. Dad bought burgers and a beer for us at Lewies before we headed home. I prodded him to tell me stories I'd heard a hundred times before about his youth on that mountain to keep the chatter light and sent out gratitude for his humility, his humor, and his company.

That night though, back on the Lovesac® with aching muscles and a mug of hot cocoa, I was somber. Fresh memories of the day filled me with a sadness. What if I couldn't do this? What if I couldn't be a skier? What if going back to the life I had just wasn't possible?

Then I knew it was true. It wasn't possible. Of course I wouldn't be able to go back to the life I had. I wasn't the same, I would never be the same. My body would never work the same way, but more than that, neither would my mind. I would never be the beautiful, outdoorsy, adventurous mountain woman I had wanted to be – I wouldn't even be able to be the woman I *had* been – because my mind and my body wouldn't let me.

I had already spent the money though, so I obliged to nearly weekly trips to the mountain and, while there was improvement, I still ended every day exhausted and frustrated with the effort. Nevertheless, weekend after weekend, my pride pushed me to first get in the car, then keep my mouth shut about wanting to go home, and then strive to make better turns in front of my father.

On one particularly fine Saturday afternoon, as we stood at the top of the run named Empress, my heart warmed at the fond memory of my favorite race course set up under the lift I'd always known as the Red Chair. It had been a beautiful Giant Slalom, designed in part by my father, and its wide turns and high speed had made it a perfect match for my strengths on skis. I remembered "packing" the course; several of us slipping down between the gates, defining the turns and taking coaching advice from my dad as we went.

"Stay high, and begin your turn above the gate," he'd tell our little group. "It'll feel too soon, but if you wait, it'll be too late. Focus on where you'll turn a few gates down from where you are." When I had the chance to ride up the chair with him before the start he'd told me about how he'd prepared for races when he was young.

"All the way up the chair I'd try to *see* myself running the course. The way my knees were bent, where I started each turn, where my poles were positioned... And when I pushed through the starting gate I tried to ski a few turns ahead of where I actually was in the course, you know what I mean?" I had nodded that day, understanding what he meant. My music teacher had told me the same thing... to read a few lines ahead on the page. But here today, with a brace on each leg, I understood his instructions in a whole new way. As we tipped our weight forward and began the first few turns, I forced myself to focus farther down the slope and plan my turn several feet before I began. I tried to see myself in my mind, knees driving forward, upper body erect and thighs pressing the ski to flex into the curve. The first turn was luxurious. Smooth and in perfect control I sailed through it to the other side of the slope and then flexed my skis again, my focus already much farther downhill. The change was incredible. Suddenly I was floating again, soaring across the surface of the snow, dancing on my skis with my heart pounding in my chest and a smile stretched wide across my face. I could hardly contain my excitement when I slipped into the line at the bottom beside my father. "That was great!" he exclaimed, almost as breathless as I, "You were really cranking on them down there. Nice job, Jaci!" My pride bubbled over and I could not speak but stood at his side, reveling in his arm around my shoulders in congratulations and grinning like a jester. The whole rest of the day I enjoyed the sport more than I had all year, and nearly as much as I had before.

FOURTEEN

It was hot for May, really hot, when my sister met me at the door of her garage, a tight smile on her face. She wanted to be happy for me. I knew that. But mostly she was scared, and I knew that too.

I had my hair pulled up in a ponytail and wore my trusty red bandana to keep the tiny hairs at the front of my head from turning into little dreadlocks. It was too hot for leather, but the plastic-armor reinforced red nylon jacket - gifted to me by a vendor years before - hung from my finger as she hoisted the heavy wood door. I grinned at the sight of it, covered in a thick layer of dust.

"Are you sure you want to do this?" she asked as I brushed off the seat and smoothed my hand over the white butterfly sticker on the fender.

"Yes. I am." I struggled to maneuver it out from between the old couch and the lawn mower.

"Here. Let me help you." She fondly brushed me aside, swung her leg over the saddle, and easily pushed and pulled the little red Buell out from the piles of junk and into the sunshine of the driveway. From the time she had outpaced me in size and strength she had taken it upon herself to watch out for me, especially after the accident. I didn't need as much help as she gave, but I knew with each gesture she was telling me she loved me, so I let her do it anyway.

I thanked her and put my jacket on. She gestured for the key and after only one sputter, it started right up.

"I love this bike," I said with a smile, almost to myself.

She got off and stood beside me in silence for a minute while the engine hummed and warmed.

"Why? Why are you doing this?" she blurted out.

"Because I love it." At the moment I could think of no other more compelling reason so I left the response hanging in the silence between us. She let it settle while she absently dusted off the seat again.

"Aren't you afraid?" The fear in her eyes was pleading with me and my heart ached to put her in such pain.

"A little, yeah. Of course. But that's why I want to do it."

She looked at me again, unconvinced and bordering on angry. "I love riding," I told her. "I don't want to give up the things I love because I'm afraid I might get hurt. I don't want to be afraid... of anything, really. For a long time there, it was scary just to walk. Stairs were terrifying! If I don't make myself stronger than the fear where will it end? Someday I'll be afraid of hiking. Or kayaking. Or rollerblading. I'll stop doing the things I love and end up living my entire life on my couch."

"Yeah, but this is a little different than hiking, Jaci."

"Not really," I tried to challenge her gently. "I could get hurt crossing the street, or falling down the stairs of my apartment, or choking on my food! Where does trust begin and end? Not your trust in me, but trust in a higher power, fate, the Universe, whatever... Trust that something outside of you is more powerful than 'careful' will ever be, and that what happens is meant to? I'm not saying people should run around inviting danger, but when my time is up, it's up, whether I'm riding a motorcycle or not."

I looked at her. She was staring straight ahead, her eyes wet. I turned off the bike and sat down on the concrete, gesturing for her to join me. She was fighting hard against the tears now, and my heart broke again.

"Jess – did I ever tell you about the helmet?" I tried hard to be gentle.

"What helmet? No, I guess not."

"That day when I got to Trevor's house and we went to get on the bike he stopped me and asked if we should wear them. I had no idea what he was talking about. I asked 'wear what?' and he said 'the helmets'. In all the years we'd been riding together we'd never worn helmets - not on the Harley anyway. I said 'No, why would we?' He shrugged and we both got on." Her brows were knit in misunderstanding when she looked at me. "After I came out of the coma, when he came to visit me in the hospital, he told me he'd had a dream while he was napping that afternoon that we were in a motorcycle accident."

She looked at me and this time I was sure she was about to cry. "You WERE in an accident! And I almost lost you!" I hugged her and felt her fight her heaving chest. "Yeah, but Jess... I think that was meant to happen." She pulled away to look at me. "And my head and my right arm were the only parts not damaged." She dragged her sleeve across her eyes and then looked at me again. "My HEAD, Jess. I was thrown from the back of Trevor's bike, into the side of a pickup truck, then landed on the pavement and was run over by a trailer - hauling a bobcat no less - that kicked me to the hill on the other side of the road.... and my head wasn't damaged at all. I was spared, even though we didn't take the "sign" because my soul wasn't done here. There's more life for me to live." Her cheeks were pink and her eyes were wet when she looked at me. I hugged her again, but she said nothing. "If I don't do this, if I surrender to fear and give up the things I love, the fear will spread and if I don't keep fighting it, it'll win. I'm already fighting it on skis, and on my bike..."

"Oh so you're going to get on a motorcycle?" she was joking, but only a little. I grinned at her.

"I'll take it slow."

She gave me that tight smile again, her eyes big. And then a long hug. "Be careful. Call me as soon as you're home, OK?"

"I'm going to be fine, Jess," I assured her, portraying more confidence than I felt.

The bike felt lighter under me than I remembered and my nerves immediately kicked into high gear. I felt my chest get tight and butterflies fluttered in my stomach. I smiled at Jess and blew her a kiss. I wrestled the bike around so I was facing down the hill out of the driveway, took a deep breath and blew it out quickly. Muscle memory took over and before I knew it I had shifted into first and was easing my Buell through the gravel alley, headed for the gas station. *I'm going to be fine. I'm going to be fine,* I assured myself as the numbers ticked by on the pump. I took long, slow, calming breaths as I waited for the filler gun to click off. The charge was $5.82. I put the gas cap on, seated my sunglasses tightly against my face and adjusted my jacket. I swung my leg over the seat and sat for a minute with the motor gently rumbling beneath me, considering my route. I wanted to be by myself. I wanted to be able to go as slow as I wanted without holding traffic up.

From here, I could take highway 16 to the cut across on Catron, and Sheridan Lake Road out to Highway 385. That sounded nice. Traffic should be light at 2 o'clock on a Thursday. I checked both ways, twice, and took to the road.

Immediately I was scared. A lot more scared than I had thought I'd be. I could feel my whole body tighten at every bump, every pothole, every place where the asphalt had cracked and been re-sealed. *What the hell am I doing?!* I thought as I headed out of town. The long straight away up to the cut across was easier and I let myself be soothed by the warmth of the sun on my skin and the smell of summer. I still loved it. Scared as hell, yes. But I still loved it. When I executed a shaky turn onto the cut across paranoia bubbled up in me again. There was more traffic than I thought, and I had completely forgotten how many tight turns were between me and the highway. Gravel on the center line and shoulder inspired thoughts of fishtailing, and visions of my body skidding along the road under my bike, my leg pinned to the ground. Just as I made it through another corner and began to relax in another short straight away, I spotted Biker Bob.

All my young life he had been there in various forms; from stuffed clothing and a painted face to a fully dressed mannequin, marking one of the tightest switch-back corners in the Black Hills. Apparently so many had been injured on this curve over the years that the owners of the home that sat squarely on the corner had put up a warning of their own. No matter his form, the doll sat astride an old rusted out motorcycle, and held a friendly sign pleading for riders to slow down. Just the sight of him rendered my whole body rigid. I had completely forgotten about this turn, but it was too late to do anything about it now. I was already 'in' the more than 90 degree uphill curve that finished with a steep, blind shot up the other side. My eyes locked on the loose stones in the shoulder, and the deep ditch beneath. I had come into the curve too fast. I wouldn't be able to make the corner. I was going down. My breath caught and I was completely paralyzed.

And then... I was through it and headed to the top of the rise on the other side. I wasn't sure how, but I'd made it. A potent mix of relief and accomplishment washed over me when I looked down the road at the next turn. My heart was still pounding when I heard my father's voice and remembered his coaching. "Where are you looking, Jaci? Don't wait until you're already in the turn to act. Don't drive off the end of the hood... Look down the run, down the road." I shifted my gaze further down the yellow line and immediately felt more capable. *I can do this.* I realized I had pulled my shoulders tight up around my ears, and took advantage of the straightaway to stretch my back tall. *I can do this*, I repeated. *I just need to focus...* Focus! Yes. Just like on my skis, where I focused mattered. I just needed to focus farther down the road, on where I wanted to go.

When I pulled out of the last turn before the intersection to Highway 385 I breathed a sigh of relief. I'd made it. I could see the stop sign where I'd turn right toward home. Shadows from huge pine trees laid across the short stretch of road toward the highway that would deliver me home. *It's fine, Jaci,* I told myself. *There's plenty of light left. You can do this.* I took the corner and relaxed. *I'm getting better at this already,* I told myself. I was on the last long stretch. Highway 44 ran down through the area known as Johnson Siding, and then... my heart froze. The bike and I continued to move forward but my mind was locked in fear. In a mile or two I would be coming up on Falling Rock, the corner where Trevor and I had gone down. Reflexively I eased off the throttle, then caught a glimpse of the traffic behind me and pushed back up to speed. My breath was shallow in my chest and my whole body was stiff. I could stop. I could turn around. But then I'd have to go back the way I came, and do the last, hardest stretch in the dark. I could take the long way home, but same thing; it would be dark. I was already wishing for a heavier sweatshirt under my jacket. And I was so close now. I eased through one corner and then another, debating my course until it was so close there really wasn't anywhere to change my mind. I sucked in a few tiny bugs in several deep breaths and reminded myself again; *I can do this*. I saw the corner coming, eased off the throttle and felt my heart pounding. I pleaded for help, desperation and fear turning to panic in my mind. *Focus down the road. I can do this. I am a good rider. I know what to do.* I sucked in a few more deep breaths through my nose, and locked my eyes on the centerline at the farthest edge of my vision, where I could see the road developing before me as I came further and further through the turn. *I can do this. I can do this.* The road seemed to arc forever and for a moment I thought I might be hypnotized by the dark asphalt rushing by beneath me when suddenly the scene before me widened and the view over the stunning Black Hills filled my vision. The grin that split my face nearly brought tears to my eyes. I looked down at the speedometer and realized I was only going 30 miles an hour. I laughed out loud and rolled on the throttle. Several cars had piled up behind me and I felt embarrassment flash through me before I wrote it off entirely and chose joy. And pride. I'd made it. I had done it. It didn't matter that I had been crawling along at a snail's pace. I had done it.

The last 20 minutes of the ride were glorious. Fear still lingered at the back of my mind, but my heart was beating fast and powerful, this time with exhilaration. I had overcome and I had survived. Again. I felt brave, and strong, and I had forgotten how nice it felt to be proud of me. I sat on the front stoop smiling around my cigarette until the whole of night had come down upon me. I had done it. Today, I was a rider again.

The Me I Was

FIFTEEN

It was crowded at the park downtown, throngs of people pushing against each other. The July sun had set long ago, but the night was warm. The last of the firecrackers lit the night sky when the three of us descended on the park. A mass of bodies surged forward and then back like the tide of the sea and my friends and me with it, floating directionless in fits of laughter and conversation. Just as we pulled to the edge of the throng to discuss our destination, he came, dancing between people stiffened in confusion and when I caught a glimpse of him, my heart jumped.

"Nichola!" my friend startled me with her summons from just behind my ear. The dancer seemed to pause mid-air, changing his direction to land facing us. "Nichola! Good to see you!" she grinned broadly. He offered only a shy smile from 6 feet up as she made quick introductions.

"It's good to see you too. There's a party at Anne's," he addressed her and stole glances at all of us. "You should come," he said enthusiastically before he joined the current moving in the other direction and danced away again. We happily obliged his invitation, jumped to the other side of the walk, and soon found ourselves following a short string of people headed up the boulevard toward Anne's.

The party was one of those incredible and rare experiences where you are fairly certain everyone around you is magic. A fire held to its place with a large iron ring sent licking flames skyward under the fluttering leaves of a tall Elm tree. People were dancing in the gravel driveway, guitars sang with the voices, sometimes with and sometimes under the din of lively conversation that sputtered and started between laughter and song lyrics.

My friends and I stayed for some time, then joined an impromptu parade heading for downtown and I did not see Nichola again. Not until late in August, when I had the least interest in seeing anyone at all.

Trevor and I had been attempting a friendship over the past two years and it was not going well. His desire – I guessed – to take care of me, forcing misunderstanding of my explicit feelings; I loved him, but I was not his. After another long, heart-wrenching argument, I had taken refuge on the concrete stoop outside the door of the ancient building I had called home for the better part of a decade. I thought I had hidden myself well, in the shadows of the streetlight that draped across the doorway.

I had only just lit my smoke when the dancer appeared and took a seat at my side. I recognized him, but I was not in the mood for company. He made small talk, I nodded and grunted appropriately, politely and stared at the night.

His true beauty escaped me then, the combination of my state and deep shadows keeping his face from me. It was not so, though, when I agreed to join him for a drink a couple days later. His eyes were intensely beautiful, the color of a thickly forested hillside with deep valleys in the corners from years of smiling. His hair was ringed with an elastic band and thick chunks of it hung in large, loose curls that he repeatedly corralled behind his ears. His smile was broad, genuine and warm but was not shared too readily and he said very little. What he did say was meaningful, interesting... or flat out hilarious. The emotion reflected in the windows of his soul was deep, and I knew very quickly he carried the woes of the earth heavy in his heart. But there was a lightness, a playfulness too, and it was not long before I was utterly captivated by him. I could see in him a power, a presence I had never known in another man. I could see in him an understanding of love and God, and life and our place in it... that I could agree with, that I had long agreed with. I could see in him a fierce moral conviction and love of play, and when I saw him in my mind, I saw his spirit shine.

I loved to be near him, I loved to listen to him talk. I loved the way he told stories, the way he learned, the way he taught. I loved that he shared my love of the outdoors, of motorcycles and skis. I loved his love of the Mother Earth, his understanding of family and his respect for women. I admired him, I respected him and it was not long before I loved him, utterly and completely.

I knew then that he was the man I had waited for, the man I had prayed for almost a year before, in a hotel room in Colorado. When Nichola touched me, I felt literally as though I were melting in his hands. When he pulled me close, I could let go of all the troubles of the day, of my life. He was my match, I was sure, and we belonged together. After only a few weeks, he wrapped all his belongings in a tarp and moved them from the room he rented, to the corner of the bedroom in my downtown apartment.

***

"Oh my gawd, Nichola! You look JUST like Brad Pitt in Snatch!" We were out for drinks on a brisk fall night and - apparently - had just run into a woman he knew in the doorway of a quiet pub. It happened a lot. He donned his sunglasses and did his best pikey impression. He did look just like Mr. Pitt. We all laughed.

"This is Jaci," he said, giving me a boyish smile.
I grinned and stretched out my hand to a heavier set woman with mousy brown hair and fire engine red lipstick. "Nice to meet you."

"Oh, so you're the flavor of the month," she said, giving me the up and down before she flipped her hair and turned away.

"What? No!" Nichola laughed uncomfortably at her back and pulled me in for a hug, burying my emotion in his chest. I put on a smile when he pulled back to look at me. Suddenly I wanted to go home. I let him order me another drink instead and took a seat in an empty booth by the windows.

I got it. I knew why women adored him and looked jealously at me when he held my hand. Not only was he beautiful, his gentle, loving soul shone out from his smile and radiated from his touch. He was friendly, outgoing, funny and kind. You knew immediately that he was different, safe. He treated women with the utmost respect... and he was a man's man. Tall, and muscular with strong hands and a full mouth framed by a short beard that mingled with the curls of his dark, shoulder length hair. He had a certain magic, and it was quickly, yet quietly, obvious. I knew she'd thought what they all probably did; I was not good enough for him. Short, stocky, pimpled...

I stared out the window at the traffic on the sidewalk and tried my best to feel comfortable. I was already losing ground fast when he returned with my drink and the woman with the red lipstick on his heels. "Nichola. I want you to meet Tessa." Nichola nodded respectfully to her, smiling, and Tessa grinned broadly. I stiffened. She was beautiful. Tall and slender, with curly brown hair to her shoulders and bright blue eyes. The two women joined us and talked – mostly to Nichola. "Tell 'im what you're doin' with the shop," the one with the red lips urged her friend.

"I'm opening my own vintage shop," Tessa addressed him with a grin. "Clothing, furniture, art..." Congratulations!" I blurted out. A pit formed in my stomach.

"It's off fourth street near the park" she said, looking at Nichola and smiling. He grinned and gave her a high five.

"Nice!" he said. My heart shrunk. I felt the zit on my cheek burning, festering, growing into a mountain right before this woman's eyes. I forced a smile, not sure what else to say and felt my whole self crumble. She was exceptional – in every way. And what was I? Boring. Broke. Insecure. Scarred. I made small talk awhile longer and excused myself to go home. Nichola did not come with me.

Self loathing flooded my mind and my heart ached more with every step, every thought. By the time I dropped myself onto the stoop and lit my last smoke of the night, I knew I would lose him to her. Even if it wasn't now, tonight... even if it wasn't her... what did I possibly have to offer that could compare with this incredible woman? All these incredible women? His whole circle of friends, every woman who had ever spoken to him had something better than I had. They were talented. Or beautiful. Or successful. Or smart. Or creative. Or interesting. Or all of those things. What did I have to offer someone as amazing as Nichola? Nothing.

I lay in bed a long time, awake, staring at the ceiling. Was it worth it? Was this kind of heartache worth real, deep love? *I could call Brad* I thought, with a moment of whimsy. Brad adored me. He had loved me for years, and professed his devotion on several occasions. It was a standing invitation, he'd said. He would do just about anything to make me happy, and had reminded me several times not only that he would, but that he could. He was very successful, and wanted nothing more than to shower me with expensive jewelry, and trips, and clothes. But I did not love him. I could not love him – not like that. Even as I thought about the life he could provide, and warmed at the memory of his sweet smile, I knew I would never consider such an arrangement. I wanted love.

I threw the covers off, shoved my feet into my shoes without socks, and shuffled down the hallway and stairs. The world was quiet and the clouds on the furthest horizon were just blushing with pink. I smoked one cigarette, and then another, before surrendering myself to awake. I hiked the stairs again for the keys to my car, grabbed my wallet, and took a cup of coffee from my favorite little shop on main street to the top of the highest point in town. The sun was only just peeking its fluid gold over the edge of the world when I put my car in park and sat on a ledge of rock with my cup and my smoke.

It was an eerie calm, an almost resigned peace that settled over me as I watched the clouds turn to flame and then die out and settle to ribbons of ash in the bright fall sky. I couldn't live like this. Insecurity was eating me alive, an acid on my soul and spirit that was breaking me down to a childish, victimized, ugly little girl. I didn't like her. I didn't like me. There it was, the truth. I didn't like me. I hadn't ever, now that I thought about it.

It didn't matter that I could ride a motorcycle again, or that I had finally mastered my bike and skis. Doing those things meant nothing. They were simply things I did – and not even well. They weren't who I was. They didn't make me special.

Suddenly I understood. All my life I had been trying to find value - something about myself that I could love - in a definition; a talent, a career, a city, a degree, a man… *That* was why I wasn't supposed to go to New York. *That* was why Denver didn't work out and school had fallen through. I had wanted those things to *make* me the kind of woman that I wanted to be, the kind of woman I could love. But I wasn't the free-spirited, adventurous, independent, outdoorsy bohemian goddess I had wanted to be. I was unattractive, insecure, scarred and scared, and I couldn't possibly love that.

I wanted to blame him for not making me feel loved, I wanted to make it his fault that I didn't feel beautiful or special. But it wasn't. It was my problem. I knew that. It had been my problem for years. I had to fix it. Now. Right now. I had to find value and beauty in myself - not in what I did or where I lived, but in who I was.

I knew then that I had to leave Nichola. I was sure I could feel my heart physically breaking at the thought, but I knew my real heart – the deep, center-of-my-soul one - would never recover if I didn't.

I had already gassed up and a second cup of coffee was steaming in the console of my car downstairs, as I shoved four or five Tshirts and sweatshirts into a bag along with jeans, socks and a toothbrush. I dug out a couple blank journals I had been given in the hospital and slid them into a messenger bag alongside my laptop. I knew if I thought about it too long my mind would win over and I would decide to stay, sheerly out of the fear that he wouldn't be here, or wouldn't want me, when I came home. I messaged Nichola to see if he could meet me for lunch and stopped at my sister's house to give her the news.

"But I thought you really liked this guy," she said in confusion.

"I did. I do," I told her and gratefully took the lit cigarette she offered me before lighting one for herself. We were back in her driveway again, this time watching the leaves blow down the alley.

"So why are you leaving again?"

I took a deep breath and had exhaled in a sigh before I realized it. "Here's the thing, Jess. He's MAGIC. Incredible. Beautiful. And I'm... I'm just not."

"Yes you are! How can you possibly say that? You're beautiful, you're smart..."

"Pffffttttthhhhh." I interrupted her. "I'm not. And even if I were," I held my hand up before she could protest. "Even if I were... I don't feel it. I feel small and ugly and scared... and I feel all those terrible things about myself more when he's around because he's so incredible, and the women that flock to him are incredible. The ugly truth is, I don't like myself very much and being with a man that I genuinely admire and love makes it all the more evident - ironically."

She stared out at the trees losing their leaves to the alley wind. "And how is this little vacation, or whatever it is you're doing, going to help you with that?" I shrugged in response. "I don't really know. I just feel the need to get away, I guess," I told her weakly. "My heart is screaming for solitude."

"You're sure it's your heart?" I nodded. "What if you're heart is wrong? What if you are supposed to stay here?"

"Oh, sister. My heart is never wrong." She looked at me a little surprised. I was a little surprised. "The way I believe - and I know it's MY belief... it doesn't work for everybody - but I believe that we are all - taken together - God." She looked surprised, again, and a little confused. "I think of God as energy - the only thing that can't be created or destroyed. It just exists, everywhere, in EVERYTHING."

She nodded almost imperceptibly and I was sure she thought I'd rather lost it. The fall sun was thin but warm on our faces and I could hear naked branches creaking above us.

"Did you know Aspen trees have connected roots?" I asked. She shook her head and looked sideways at me. "Nichola told me that. He said they are one of the largest organisms on the planet for that reason. I've always loved the Aspen and Birch sprinkled through the Hills - well you know." She grinned and nudged me.

"Tree hugger" she whispered. I grinned.

"I think we're like the Aspen and Birch trees; our souls, our energies, are - taken together - the largest force of light and love and power and grace in all the universes. Together, we're God."

"ALL souls?" she asked, skeptically, and after a moment I knew what she was getting at.

"Yes," I told her. "I think each of us chooses to send a part of our soul - our "seed", our "son" - to live on this earth plane in human form, to learn, evolve, and teach. Even those souls that come into this world as the makers of "evil" are valuable - maybe even more so - because they said 'I will go. I will live a life void of real love or happiness, filled with anger and sadness and hatred and pain so that the rest of you can live in – and understand - the light.'" We both sat in silence for a moment. I wasn't sure what she thought of my theory, but I knew it didn't matter because she loved me perfectly.

"I think as we grow, we bring the lessons learned here back to the 'forest' or whatever for all to share. I believe our higher selves are constantly sending messages and resources here to guide and support us – through our hearts. And our guts. But mostly our hearts." I realized I was narrating my theory for the first time, almost working through the ideas as I spoke. "We're taught to value brains over gut feelings and think things out rather than feel them out, but maybe we were given five senses and a brain that can't feel for a reason," I mused. "There are actually more nerve endings in our gut than in our brain. So it makes sense to me that our higher power would connect and communicate with us through our bodies. Doesn't the bible even call our bodies temples?" She nodded in concession. "Then of course I 'feel' God, in my heart, in the 'temple' he/she/it built. Not 'think' him, or it, or whatever." She shrugged, almost in agreement. "I think we get a gut feeling because we *know*. The soul – the God - inside us is screaming and we're suffocating it with antacid and Internet research." She laughed out loud, now, and I was grateful. "I guess what I'm saying is, I think that little part of God that's in all of us lives in our hearts - in my heart. My real, true, heart-and-soul heart. So if my heart wants something, it's the right thing."

She took a deep breath and drew shapes in the gravel with the heel of her shoe.

"Where are you going to go? Where will you stay?"

"I don't know yet, honestly."

"You should at least get your first hotel booked. And tell me where you're going!" I giggled at my little sister, my heart warmed by her concern. She smiled.

"Look, Jess, I know this isn't probably the way most people would handle this, but I really want to just go and see where the road takes me. Life is too short to do what I *should*. I want to do what I *LOVE*. I want to LOVE my life. I feel like this trip is a chance for me to learn how to do that, and I think a part of that is trusting my instincts, just getting in the car, and turning left when I feel like turning left or right when I feel like turning right, know what I mean?"

She nodded in resignation, knowing full well that once I decided to do something like this, there was no changing my mind. We hugged, I promised to call or email once in awhile to tell her where I was, and she told me with a grin that I'd better come home. I gave her a half-smile and told her I couldn't make any promises.

I fought back tears all the way to the restaurant where I met Nichola.

"Hi," he said, brightly, cautiously. I could tell he was gauging me.

"Hi," I smiled.

After the waitress came I broke the silence that fell between us with my news. "I'm going on a little trip." He knit his brow.

"Where?"

"I don't know yet. West, I think. I might head for the coast."

He looked at me quizzically. "When? Why? What's this about?" Tenderness and alarm shown in his eyes and I was reminded that he really did care about me. I wanted to cave. I wanted to tell him I was kidding, and let's get a sandwich, shall we? But I knew it wasn't his love I needed. Even if he treated me as if I were the only woman in the world, even if he made me feel like a goddess, it wouldn't really change anything - for me. I didn't want to need to be loved. I wanted to truly love me. My heart was crumbling all over the table when I smiled at him.

"Actually, my car is packed. I was planning on leaving today. Like, when we're done here..." This time he looked genuinely alarmed.

"Is this because I never really moved in? Or because I didn't come home last night? I'll unpack. It's not that I don't want to, I'm just lazy." He reached across the table for my hands. "And last night I just fell asleep on the couch in Troy's apartment." He was nearly pleading with me now. A tear broke through my dam and slid down my cheek.

"No, no... it has nothing to do with you unpacking." I grinned broadly despite my stinging eyes. "That's not to say I wouldn't really like it if you did. That pile of stuff in the corner is driving me crazy." We shared a shallow giggle and then the silence again. "I figured you were at Troy's last night..." I said, after a lengthy pause. He looked at me with a boyish, expectant smile.

"Nichola, it's me. I just... I've lost myself. And you, my friend, are very distracting." I hoped the deep love I had for him shown in my eyes along with playful desire. "I just have to do this."

"How long will you be gone?"

I shrugged in response. "I'll definitely be home before Thanksgiving..."

"Thanksgiving?!" He quickly recovered himself and smiled. "It's ok." He seemed heartened. "I can be patient. I'm Mister Patient." The dam broke and twin tears spilled and ran like rivers to my chin. I wiped at them shyly and grinned at him. We ignored the topic over brunch and delayed paying the check until we could no longer.

The afternoon was unusually warm and overcast when he walked me to my car. It took all my nerve, but I did not cry when I hugged him, got in my car, and headed west.

Jaclyn Lanae

SIXTEEN

The prairie around me quickly gave way to mountains, their clouded peaks still – or already – covered in snow. The sun was no match for the cool blanket of moisture and I was reminded of *America the Beautiful* "…purple mountain majesties, above the fruited plain." Sprawling fields on both sides of the road had been harvested, stumps of corn stalks and wheat basked in the deep golden shade of evening sunlight and I watched the mountains move and shift before me.

My heart ached. I wanted to turn around and go running back, to wrap all my happiness up in Nichola. I wanted to take shelter in his arms and feel the happy, and not worry whether or not it would last or if I would be OK. I knew if I were gone very long, he would be too by the time I got home. How does someone that beautiful, that charismatic, that friendly and loving and kind stay single? Especially when he is surrounded by beautiful, talented, passionate, successful, free-spirited women? My heart got heavier. I couldn't compete, and I knew it. He would not be there waiting for me when I came home, I was sure. But I knew I had to do this. I had to put myself first, and I had to figure out how to be OK with me - LOVE me, even. Boring, broke, plain, broken, me. If I turned around now, I would be denying what I KNEW I knew. I'd be denying my very heart.

***

I spent the first night in a Gillette, Wyoming hotel and ate IHOP for breakfast for the first time since Charlie and I had been stranded on the coast. It wasn't delicious, but it brought back fond memories of our adventure, and our time together. I didn't miss him, I realized, as much as I missed the woman I had felt like in front of him. It had been easy to feel beautiful and incredible in front of Charlie; he'd thought I was those things. We weren't meant for each other though, and I knew it. We didn't have a whole lot in common, and I wasn't in love with him. I was sure he wasn't in love with me, either. Especially not now. I grinned at the thought. Oh, he wouldn't have minded my scars.... but I couldn't imagine he would have been OK with the 'new' me.

I, like Charlie, was raised in a very traditional Roman Catholic home. We prayed together before school each morning, before each meal, and before bed every night. We said rosaries and attended church and catechism classes. I read the bible cover to cover, and was elected to the National Catholic Youth Congress. That's how we'd met, in fact, Charlie and I.

I smiled again at the thought as I got in my car and headed west. Wow. I had been a completely different kind of person all those years ago. But that kind of God had never really worked for me.

Besides, I liked the way I thought about God now... and the whole spirituality I had built for myself. I didn't think other versions were wrong, just different. It made sense to me that God would be different for all of us, that each of us would find the spirituality or religion or ceremony or whatever we needed to understand a higher power or our role in the world in a way that was real to us personally. I'd always thought perhaps the Christian's Noah's ark story was the same as the Native Americans' Turtle story – each expressed differently based on what the people could understand. Maybe the bible story of the Tower of Babel was not so much about the diversification of language, as the diversification of what God is to each of us - individual people and cultures as a whole.

If I believed God was a part of me, of all of us, should that not be where I put all my focus? On me? On the God in me? *I am not God, but God is me.* Maybe my most important duty in my time on this planet - my real, deep purpose - was to really understand and LOVE myself and in doing so, understand and love "God".

I was growing road weary and hungry when Ashton, Idaho blazed on the green highway sign under my headlights. *It definitely falls into the "sleepy" category*, I thought as I crawled down what appeared to be the only main street. I checked into a hotel on the far edge, dropped my duffel on a dated, mauve colored bed spread, and walked across the street to the only real restaurant I had seen. I wanted to spoil myself a little; A good pasta dish, a glass of wine... The maitre'd escorted me to a sweet little table for two, snugged up against the towering stone wall of the huge fireplace that sat front and center. She politely removed one set of silverware and I felt the eyes of the whole place on me as I draped my jacket over the back of my chair and took a seat. *I guess it's probably not the norm for a town like Ashton to have a lot of tourist traffic on a Tuesday in October*, I thought as I worked to ignore the attention and appear, at least, comfortable in my own skin.

I immersed myself in a study of the wine menu and when my waitress still had not come I resorted to gazing around the room. I had read and re-read every quote on every little wooden sign in the building by the time the waitress arrived. "I love to cook with wine. Sometimes I even put it in the food." and "If you're smoking in here, you'd better be on fire!" hung crookedly on either side of the hallway toward the kitchen. "Your smile looks great on you. You should wear it more often!" hung on the wall next to my table and I thought briefly about how odd it would be to sit here smiling at no one and nothing. I knew it hadn't been that long, but it had felt like forever when the waitress finally came. I ordered a glass of the house Merlot and an Alfredo dish, and as soon as she left I was searching for the little wooden signs again.

Why? Why was I so uncomfortable? I should be able to just sit here comfortably. Truly strong, truly beautiful, truly independent women could, I was sure. I wasn't strong. *Clearly*, I thought, bitterly. I was uncomfortable, and shy, and a little scared. I tried to push the sense of despair out of my mind and enjoy my wine. I studied the stones in the wall next to me and thought how lovely it would be if people looked at me because I was interesting and beautiful. Maybe an attractive young man would approach me, ask me where I was from and where I was headed. I'd tell him that I wasn't sure yet. He'd be smitten with my fierce independence and quiet demeanor. He'd ask if he could take me out for a drink. I'd say yes and we'd go dancing and when I left him, later, alone in the night he would always think of me as the beautiful, mystery woman that was just too wild and free to be held by any place, or any man. I was driving off into the sunrise in an old truck with the imaginary man in the imaginary rear view mirror when the waitress interrupted my story and graciously delivered my meal. I ate absently, wandering around in my mind, looking for the thing that would get me to "ok". By the time I had scraped my plate I was no closer than when I had arrived. I left a good tip and escaped back to the hotel.

The deck outside the doors of my room was just wide enough that I could sit against the wall with my legs straight out and barely touch the railing on the other side. I watched the smoke from my cigarette drift through the bars and up toward the moon. Why couldn't I be the kind of woman that just WAS magic, the kind of woman that Nichola deserved, the kind of woman I wanted to be? Instead I had to somehow learn to be ok with the me that existed; boring, scarred, and self-conscious. How? How was I supposed to do that? How was I supposed to learn to love myself when I wanted to be someone else?

I looked down at my legs, felt the little muffin top pushing out over the waist of my jeans, and wiped at a tear that I had let slide. I felt the sting of a new pimple growing on my chin and wallowed in my misery. I hated that I had to give Nichola up for this. I hated that I was ugly. I hated that I had nothing special to offer him or the world. I wasn't even trying to be dramatic… I could genuinely think of nothing about myself that was truly wonderful, nothing I could truly love. My heart ached and my cheeks were a mess of tears. Eventually I put out my smoke and went inside where I fell asleep fully clothed, sprawled sideways across a thin mattress.

**

Burnt coffee and a banana was all the breakfast I could consider from the hotel lobby and I was just sipping the first from the paper cup as the sun painted its gold on the windows of the boutique across the street. I felt better this morning, a little, anyway.

The day was bright, and traffic was light. I made it a point to stay off the interstates and just listen to where my heart wanted to go. It seemed like the first step in really knowing and loving who I was, was to know and follow my heart. At every turn I tried to get quiet, listen, hear my soul... and at every turn I seemed to run into roadblocks. Literally. First I ran into such heavy construction the road was fully closed. Dead end. Another road just kind of stopped after awhile, and when I consulted my map, I couldn't find it at all. It just ceased to exist. A third took me right along the interstate. After an hour of sitting in traffic on yet another gravel road busy with construction, waiting for the lead car to come and retrieve the short line that had accumulated, I surrendered to frustration and laid my head in my hand against the glass of the driver's window. I was empty. I was lost.

I wasn't even quite sure where I was when I saw the first green signs shine in my headlights and I didn't care. I was in Montana, and that was good enough for me. After the day I'd had I decided I could go no longer sitting in the car and paid for four nights in an ancient hotel.

The TV didn't work very well and the room stunk of age but it didn't matter. I ate strawberries that had been baking in the sun on my passenger's seat and were likely hours from "bad", and stared at the dingy yellow walls. I missed Nichola. Again. Still.

Shaking my head as though to loose the thought I sat back on the peony painted bed spread and worked to quiet my mind. What the hell had happened today? Why couldn't I hear myself, my heart? I had always had great intuition. Long before I could drive I was able to guide my mother home in the middle of the night from a campground I'd never been to before. I could just 'sense' my way. Here I was, decades later, and lost in almost every sense of the word. What was wrong with me? I felt like I had just a few years ago, again scraping the bottom. Only this time it wasn't about money or a job... although that played a part. Even if they wanted me back, the motorcycle dealership couldn't save me from this, not this time. This ache, this emptiness was deeper.

I lay there for awhile, staring at the walls, pining for the woman I wanted to be. I thought of Nichola again, and felt my heart break. He was probably laughing over a beer with a friend, probably surrounded by bohemian goddesses of art, and dance, and music. He was that kind of man, and he deserved that kind of woman. I told my heart to let go of him and lay back on the mattress with a rumbling stomach. *The strawberries might have been bad...* was the last thought that skimmed across my consciousness before I gave in to sleep.

***

The only coffee shop in town didn't serve breakfast, but they had internet service. The pecan vanilla scone from a box on the counter would have to suffice. I dropped the wrapper in the wastebasket by the door where I sat, steam rising next to my screen from a too tall Americana with too much syrup and too little cream. I sent my sister a message, telling her I was ok and felt pangs of desire – I wanted to go home. I didn't even really want to go home – I wanted to fall into Nichola's arms and find Happy-Ever-After... wherever that happened to be. I knew I couldn't. It wouldn't happen that way. Besides, I had paid for three more nights.

I pushed the screen against the keys and the thought out of my mind, and tried to focus on the moment I was in. Beautiful drawings in mismatched frames lined the wood paneled walls. Some were hung without glass, unleveled, and without uniform spacing, but the work inside each was truly awe-inspiring. Impossibly detailed woodland scenes, every tiny branch and leaf and blade of grass purposefully placed. I stood to inspect further and was struck dumb with the realization that each piece of work was delicately sketched on a napkin. The barista must have heard my quiet gasp. "It's for sale," he said, gruffly. I glanced around the otherwise empty room and blushed at his awareness of my reaction. "5 bucks."

"Oh, they're worth WAY more than that," I gushed before 'shy' caught up and I had to fight the desire to flat run to my seat. He chuckled, low and quiet.

"There's a pile of 'em back here. I should just pay people to take 'em," he said with a hint of softness in his voice.

"Are these yours?" I asked, incredulous and then immediately hoped he hadn't noticed my surprise. Somehow the thin Tshirt he was wearing over his pot belly that hovered on inappropriately transparent, his thick five o'clock shadow, and deeply lined features hadn't screamed "artist". But, now that I looked at him for awhile, I could see it, I guessed.

"Gets a little boring around here," he said, as though apologizing for the decor.

"It's beautiful," I said, surprised at his demeanor, and his talent. "It really is." He looked up at me for a moment and I was certain I saw pride flash across his face.
He came out from behind the counter and needlessly wiped off a couple tables as he spoke. "Where you from?"

"South Dakota," I said, suddenly not sure whether I was really safe.

"Whatcha doin' out here?"

"Just traveling through, I guess."

"By yourself?" I looked outside for a minute, working on a response that would be both honest and not a 'stupid-girl' move that would get me hung up in the freezer I assumed was in the back. Before I could answer he knew the truth, and my fear.

"Oh, I ain't nothin' to worry 'bout," he said, and somehow I believed him. "But I ain't sayin' I'm not surprised. Girl like you, out here alone..." I wasn't quite offended, but a little put-off and I wasn't sure why. "Don't you got a boyfriend or somethin' to come along with you?" I shook my head and let a hint of playful distrust cross my face.

"What brought ya out here?" he repeated his question.

"Oh," I stalled, and then surrendered to my gut feeling that he was just a lonely old man who ran a little coffee shop. He probably saw a few visitors in the morning and a few dozen teenagers at Friday Open Mic nights, and was just anxious to talk to someone from "outside", I reasoned. "I guess I don't really know. I'm looking for something, I suppose, but I'm not quite sure what." He was working his way slowly toward me, attempting to look nonchalant and failing miserably, wiping down spotless tables as he came. I was touched by his shyness.

"Can I get you a re-fill? This one's on the house."

I grinned, gave him a guarded, playful nod, and when he brought back my second Americana he took half a seat at my table and fumbled with his towel while he talked. Apparently, we were about to be friends.

By the time he'd offered me a third refill, he had told me about his wife who had passed away unexpectedly several years before, and that the coffee shop had been her dream. He hated coffee, he confessed, or espresso at least, but she had loved it, and he didn't really know what else to do without her around, so he'd kept it open. "It was pretty bad coffee there for awhile. Never occured to me to have her teach me how to do it, you know." I could see that enough time had passed that he had learned to keep his eyes from misting, but the break in his heart still shown on his face. He had loved her. I grinned.

"Well, it's pretty damn good now." He snorted, but I could see pride in his eyes. And I hadn't lied.

"Mostly it just means I don't get out of here much anymore," he said. "But I don't mind. Gives these kids something other than that damn Marijuana to do around here." At this I laughed out loud, nearly spitting my coffee all over him, and I caught him chuckling.

"So what do you do out in So Dak?"

"Well, not a whole lot at the moment, I guess."

"Trust fund baby?"

"Oh, no... Just kind of between gigs right now. I'm not sure what I want to do. I've always liked to write, but..."

He nodded the familiar nod of a person looking upon a wanna-be; someone with a passion and no money or time to waste both on. I felt myself bristle at the perceived judgment and then sink into full embarrassment that I had nothing more proud to offer this stranger on my resume. Heavy silence fell between us. I glanced awkwardly at my computer a few times and then outside. He worried his towel until I was sure it would begin to fray before my very eyes.

"Sure is nice out."

"Yeah. It is. In fact, I should probably get going, see what I can see of your little town."

"Oh, honey, if you walked down here from the hotel you've seen all of our little town there is to see. The rest of it you can see from the sidewalk." Suddenly he brightened, then tempered his enthusiasm. "Wanna sit outside?"

I hesitated only a moment and then surrendered. I wasn't sure what I was looking for or where I would find it, but I was pretty sure it wasn't driving around and outside of sitting on the bench at the park, this was probably my best option anyway.

The sun was warm, welcoming, and the breeze carried just a touch of sorrow for the summer passing. Leaves had turned and were falling, dancing merrily down the street gutters. I wrestled my bag, laptop, book, notebook, pen and cup of coffee out onto the tipsy little bench under the awning outside the front door and settled my things. When I looked up, I could see that he was right. From our vantage at the top of the hill we could very literally see the edges of town before, and to the right and left of us. It was a sweet picture; manicured lawns and very slow moving cars, people sitting on corner benches or under trees. He told me a little about the place, about how he and his wife had come to live here back when they were kids in love. They'd had a son, but he'd gone to Utah to get married and work in insurance. David was his name, after his father. I grinned at the subtlety of his introduction.

"Jaci" I said, and offered my hand. He took it strongly, but was careful not to squeeze. He looked at me for a moment.

"How does a person go about looking for something when they don't know what it is?" he blurted out as though he'd been holding the question in for awhile now. I laughed out loud. He smiled awkwardly.

I looked at him and grinned, shook my head and shrugged. "I don't know. I just know I wasn't finding it where I was." Nichola's hug skipped across my memory and I felt myself sadden before I shook it off and gave David senior my attention.

"What's 'it'?" he asked. I shrugged again.

"I know it sounds crazy..." I measured my words, at first, unsure just how much to trust this stranger. I told my mind the messages it was sending me about the possible danger were just regurgitated fear that wasn't even my own. "I just... I wasn't right... or something...." I stalled. He let his silence ask for more information. I stared out toward the last house on the last street in front of us.

"Are you ready for this? I mean do you really want to hear 'my story'?"

"Well, I aint got nuthin' better to do." I smiled at him. He leaned in as though to whisper to me. "I got beer and wine in there too, you know." I laughed aloud again, and quickly decided that two o'clock in the afternoon was a perfectly appropriate time to drink wine when you were on vacation, and I kind of was, and I could walk to the hotel, and I didn't have anything important to do anyway...

"Pinot Noir is my favorite," I pretend-whispered back.

He came back a moment later with a glass and a bottle, a corkscrew and a beer. He turned his open sign off and stared off at the autumn sun soaking the horizon while I opened the bottle and poured myself a glass. We sat in silence awhile while I struggled to start the conversation again. I wanted to tell him, suddenly. All of it. Because I could get it all out in the open, and hear another perspective, and then walk away from him and neither of us would ever have to speak of it again. I would never have to run into him and know that he knew - about my crazy, my insecurities, my weaknesses.

"Well?" he said to the empty street in front of us. I snickered and gave him an uncertain smile.

"Really?"

"I told you 'bout Nancy. And David Jr...." I shrugged, took a big swig from my glass, and stared over the rooftops to the wide, wheat-colored plain and sighed.

"I guess, it's just... I just..." I shook my head and started again. "I think I'm falling in love with this guy," I said, startling myself with my frankness. "But the thing is he's beautiful. And the trouble with beautiful people is..."

"You feel ugly around them?" I was surprised by his insight and understanding, and surprised that I hadn't thought of it that way before.

"Yeah, I guess," I said, slowly, and took another sip. "And even that would be OK, except that there are all these beautiful, amazing women around him that are not only gorgeous on the outside, but they really have their shit in a pile, know what I mean?" That sent his belly chuckling again, so I excused myself for my own foul mouth without apologizing to him. "And here I am, this mess of a woman - no job, no goal, really... no talent... and I'm not really a pretty girl. I'm built like a tree. I have legs like stumps. When I try to cross them I kind of have to fling one up there and then finish the job with my hands... I really have no business even attempting it..." He was really laughing now and I realized I was enjoying this. It was nice to get it all out in the open instead of letting it spin around in my mind, and laughing at myself made it seem ok to be this nuts. "I have pimples all over my face and I'm short and I'm not at all graceful...."

"Well don't you go thinking I'm a danger to you or anything, but you ain't no ugly girl either," he said, grinning and wiping at tears in his eyes. I giggled.

"Well, thank you, but you can't see the really ugly parts." He was still smiling when he gave me a skeptical look and I indulged myself in my desire to tell him about it.

"I was in this crazy motorcycle accident a couple years ago, and I have all these scars..."

"Oh, they can't be that bad," he interrupted. I yanked up my pant legs in defiance, exposing misshapen legs, one larger than the other, and mostly covered in lumpy skin grafts. He cocked his head to the side and raised his eyebrows in concession.

"But you're a sweet kid..."

"Yeah, well..." I pushed my pant legs back down and sat back in my chair. "That's the thing. I don't know if that's enough, by itself."

We both watched the 'closed' signs come on in the windows of the businesses across from us for a long minute. I refilled my glass and swirled the rich red color around just to watch it splash the sides.

"If the guy is any good, he'll love you anyway," he said, finally. I nodded. There was truth to his statement, but it felt hollow. Nichola *was* 'good'. My scars didn't bother him and neither did my inflamed skin, and those things made me certain he could see my very soul. But that wasn't enough. I didn't want to be loved 'anyway'... I wanted to be loved 'because'. And, more importantly, I wanted to love me.

"I just feel like I don't have anything to offer," I said. "Even if he wasn't beautiful..." I turned in my seat to face him, grateful for the chance to get the cess pool of thoughts out of my mind and clear my head. "I always wanted to be a really amazing woman, you know? Almost magic... the kind of woman who sort of floats through the world blissfully happy, doing her own thing, not needing anyone or anything." He chuckled softly and I was reminded how silly I must sound. A silly little insecure girl getting drunk on his porch. I blushed in the waning light cast by dusk gathering on the horizon. "I guess I just wanted to be special... or something."

Now he turned and looked fully at me in the shadows collecting on our faces. "Didn't you say you was here alone?" My heart caught in my throat and I nearly dropped my glass. I nodded weakly and muttered. "That's pretty damn brave in my opinion. Especially for a not-ugly girl." He grinned and I let a breath of relief escape, softening.

"Thanks, David," I said with a giggle. He filled my glass again and we listened to the chorus of crickets for awhile.

"What happened?" he asked. I looked at his profile quizzically for a moment before I understood what he was referring to.

"Oh! The accident you mean." I took a deep breath and another sip. It wasn't that I didn't like talking about it. I did, actually. Sometimes it sparked great conversations and other incredible stories of survival. Other times, though, as soon as I told them the tale, they sort of ran away. Maybe not literally, physically, but people sometimes shut down, as if it was too much, too personal or something.

"I don't think anyone will really know... but I was riding with my boyfriend at the time, and we came into a really tight corner on kind of a narrow highway. There was a truck pulling a bobcat on a trailer in the oncoming lane... the theory is I was thrown off the back of my boyfriend's motorcycle and into the side of the truck - which is what broke all the bones in the left side of my body... and when I hit the ground the trailer he was pulling ran over my legs - which shredded off most of the skin and tore the femoral artery." I could see David shaking his head in my periphery and I sat in the heavy silence, unsure what to say, or what his response would be.

"You mad at him?"

"Who?"

"Your boyfriend." He glanced at me sideways.

"Oh, no. Not at all! And he's not my current boyfriend..." I trailed off.

"You don't have to tell me about it." David mumbled as though he felt like he was prying.

"Oh, I don't mind at all. I like talking about it, actually, to people who are interested at least. It's just... I just...." I took a breath to collect myself and started again. "The guy was an excellent rider. Still is, I think. Incredibly talented. I trusted him completely and I would again. We even rode together after I got out of the hospital." I took another breath, trying to get to my point before I lost my nerve. "You see, David, I think that our souls come here to learn something, and that part of us draws to us certain experiences... opportunities to learn. I think, on some level, my soul asked for this. I think it's good. I think ultimately I'll be a better person because of it. I honestly feel sorry for Trevor... I'm sure he felt responsible somehow, but in truth I think his soul agreed to bear the burden in order to give me such a tremendous gift." I remembered the first breaths of fresh air from my wheelchair and instinctively took a deep breath savoring the crisp smell of fall.

He said nothing and sat quite still for a moment, gazing out into the night. "That's the part that always makes me sound crazy," I nearly whispered. The breeze pushed a napkin across the sidewalk in front of us and he got up to collect it and gave it a proper home in the sealed trashcan at the end of the porch.

"You have an amazing attitude, Jaci." I gave him a half smile and kept quiet, certain I'd made him uncomfortable. Several more long minutes passed before he drained the last of his third beer and looked at me. "I don't know how you do it. I'm still mad at God for taking Nancy from me so soon." I was struck dumb by his sudden revelation and could not make my tongue work in my mouth. He almost smiled at me before he excused himself from the conversation. "I s'pose I better get on home and get some dinner in me. I gotta be back here at 5:30." I smiled.

"Me too. I mean, I better go eat something. I don't have to be back here, of course." He shook his head, a crooked smile on his face.

I'd only had a couple of glasses over the course of the last few hours, but it felt like a full bottle in my empty stomach and I could feel the buzz creeping in on me. I wanted to go home, but not hungry so I called the steakhouse from David's porch and ordered a Gorgonzola salad that I could pick up on the way back to the hotel. David emptied the rest of the bottle into a super-sized Styrofoam to-go cup and delivered it to me while I sat smoking and staring out at the emerging stars. "You walk safe, there, little miss." I grinned shyly and nodded, taking the cup. I wanted to thank him for listening to me ramble on, but didn't know how so I slung my laptop bag over my shoulder and hugged him instead. He patted my back like I remembered my grandfather doing when I was a child and it was comforting.

The salad was especially delicious and came with a cup of broccoli cheese soup and a dinner roll, all of which I practically inhaled in front of a fuzzy black and white screen before I took my to-go cup out onto the little picnic table in the tiny patch of grass near the parking lot with a pack of cigarettes and a notebook. I was embarrassed in front of myself for the way I had talked on and on about my selfish problems with David. I didn't know why I felt the way I did with him... and I had no idea why I felt guilty about it. I wrote furiously, working the thoughts out on paper, eventually concluding that I had rambled on because he felt safe, and that I felt guilty because I had done all the talking, babbling on about God as though I had some special perspective or something. But, I reasoned, it seemed like he had enjoyed it. He had opened up too, a little... I smoked the last one of the night and headed for bed.

***

The next morning he made my tall Americana a Venti at no additional charge and sent me on my way with an orange and a piece of biscotti. The shop was busy and I had no intention of spending another day on his porch so I asked the woman sweeping the sidewalk in front of her jewelry and gift store for directions to the park. She laughed.

"Oh honey... it's just at the other end of the street. Keep going down this way, about five more blocks. You can't miss it." I thanked her and wandered on, and found the end of the street opened up into a block of well maintained greenish grass, lightly sprinkled with fallen leaves and sporting an empty swing-set and slide. The remaining leaves of the oak trees above shook and quivered in even the slightest breeze and I could smell the last of someone's overnight fire drifting through town. Clouds gathered on the farthest edges of the horizon and I figured I had three solid hours before I would have to go back to the room to stay out of the rain.

For some time I just sat, trying to quiet my mind and really live in the place and moment I was in. It had been months since I'd really spent any time alone - the last time must have been in the hospital, and the last time I'd done so without the distraction of pain... I couldn't remember. At least months before that.

Eventually I surrendered and let my mind wander to the night before. I felt less bad this morning about my conversation with David. I was on vacation, kind of, and if I wanted to drink wine on the porch with a near stranger, well, that was my prerogative. There was nothing wrong with our chat... I liked that he thought I was brave, and independent... And then I realized why I had felt so good talking to David. I felt like he had seen me the way I wanted to be seen; interesting, not-ugly, maybe even spiritual... He had spoken to me as though he were interested in me, as a person. He treated me as though my perspective, the way I thought or acted or believed about the world, was valuable. It felt good and what was wrong with that? As soon as I had the thought I knew exactly what was wrong with that; it came from outside. There wouldn't always be a "David". Then what? I couldn't spend my life running around looking for people to validate me, to make me feel important or interesting or happy... I wouldn't want to anyway, I reasoned. How exhausting! Imagine running around constantly trying to find someone who liked me. And how defeating to have to get that kind of love, kindness and validation from outside.

HOW? I threw my head back and silently screamed up to the heavens. HOW DO I LEARN TO LOVE MYSELF? I had almost thought I would actually get some kind of audible message, but after the moment passed and stirring leaves were the only sound, I sat back up in defeat.

My growling stomach snapped my wandering mind back to the park bench. I could think of nothing on the menu at either the steak house or the coffee shop that sounded good so I set off in search of a grocery store. I didn't really know where I was going, but I figured I couldn't possibly get lost in a town with only one streetlight. Besides, the walk sounded nice. And it was. It was nice to be anonymous again, a feeling that was among my favorite parts of travel. It wasn't long before I had walked the better part of an hour. It couldn't be the main store, I was sure, but tucked behind the tire place on the other side of town was a hometown market. I dug out my re-useable bag to the surprise of the cashier at the checkout and bagged a container of strawberries, several avocados, a couple bags of nuts, a box of crackers, a block of cheese, and a bag of granola. The gas station down the street had single serving containers of yogurt and when I got my change after purchasing two, I left a quarter in the penny cup for six packets of salt I took from the deli's condiment station. Back outside I was suddenly lost. The spot where I stood was the peak of the hill and the street I was on dropped away on both sides to parts of town I could not see. I knew I needed to get down to the bottom of the hill but had no idea at all which way to go. I stood for a moment or two debating my course, then headed down the hill past a flower shop and the post office. Several blocks in I decided I had gone the wrong direction, but rather than hike back up the hill, I guessed that if I took the next couple of lefts I would wind up on the other side of it, heading toward the park, and eventually my hotel. An hour later I was still quite lost when I felt the first drops fall from the sky. It must have been well close to three o'clock and I was nearly dripping wet when I finally turned a corner and recognized my surroundings as the end of the main street - the wrong end. I crossed the street to avoid passing directly in front of David's coffee shop mostly because I couldn't wait to get out of my wet clothes and lose my mind in television.

By the time it was truly evening, I had enjoyed a hot shower and was lying on the bed watching what I could of a fuzzy screen. My hair was wrapped in a towel that doubled for a pillow and in the quiet moments I could hear the sound of my clothes dripping into the tub. When I could stand the TV no more I dressed myself in my pajamas, let out my hair, and took the last of my to-go cup wine outside. My legs ached as I lowered myself to the stiff outdoor carpet that covered the balcony and stuck them out in front of me. What a day. I wondered, fleetingly, if my monumental effort would translate to weight loss. *Not likely*, I thought with resignation. I was well aware that I wasn't obese, or anything, but that truth did little to soothe my insecurities about my body. *If you were a little straighter and more evenly shaped* I thought, absently massaging my throbbing quadriceps, *and a little smaller...* The thought triggered a memory and suddenly I was back in the hospital, Dr Kastr at my bedside, leaning over me and smiling.

"Yes, I probably did put your ankle on crooked," he'd joked. "Everything was broken on that side, so I just kind of had to size it up," he squatted down in demonstration, took my foot in his hand, and closed one eye, "and stick the pin in." He'd feigned pushing something through my ankle joint. My parents and I had laughed. "You're lucky you have an ankle at all," he'd said, the humor falling from his tone and face. "Honestly, if your legs had been smaller, less muscular, they'd probably have been completely torn off." He'd looked at me somberly, and then smiled. I remembered feeling flattered, somewhat, and my father laughing nervously.

I've always hated these legs, I thought, looking down at my hand massaging my thighs. They weren't pretty before, and now... I touched the depressions from the Fixator screws through my pajama pants, and felt the skin grafts stretched tight over what had been gaping holes. *At least they're starting to fill in a little, I thought. Hell, at least they're here.* I thought of my mother and my heart swelled with gratitude. *Thank God for her! I'm lucky to have legs at all, really,* I thought, and then was suddenly overcome. Exhaustion or the wine, or the thought of what my life might have been like, or the combination of the three sent tears of gratitude down my cheeks. Suddenly I felt awful for the way I had thought about my body all these years. I had hated it. And for what? My body was incredible! Look what it had survived! This rugged container was allowing me to live. And maybe most importantly, it was the container for my soul. Every meal I tasted, every embrace I shared, every tickle of joy or happiness was possible because of that one simple truth. I was alive – in this body. I would not be able to live here, touch, taste or feel without it. I would never have known the decadence of good chocolate, or how nice it felt to relax with a glass of wine and a good book. I would never have known how air smelled, or how bark felt if I had not been contained in a vessel that could touch and taste and smell and feel. *I'm so sorry* I told my legs and arms, running my hands over them as though I were applying a healing lotion. *I'm so sorry I have been angry, even mean, all these years. Thank you, for taking care of me anyway, for doing such a good job of carrying me around and helping me to experience life.*

The next morning I took my yogurt, granola, and strawberries back to the park and listened to the birds and squirrels preparing for the winter season while I ate. It seemed like I'd been here for weeks. I thought about Nichola, and this time I did not push it away. I cared about him. A lot. For a moment I wasn't sure why a sane person would leave someone they loved that much. And then I thought about how small and insecure I felt when I left and remembered why.

"Mind if I sit here?" the voice above and behind me startled me so much I nearly jumped off the bench. When I turned around I saw David's face behind me. He had a large Styrofoam cup for himself and thrust another at me. "Free refills on Thursdays," he said with a coy smile. "Pam over at the hotel said she'd seen you here yesterday.... so I took a chance. Can I sit?"

I gratefully accepted the warm cup and nodded.

"I's actually kinda surprised you're still here. It don't take three days to see Miles City."

I giggled. "Oh, I know," I said with a playful don't-I-know-it attitude and it was his turn to chuckle. "I leave in the morning." The silence that fell between us was less awkward than it was heavy, a sadness not well understood between two brand new friends.

"Going back to your boy?"

I shrugged. "I don't know yet. I don't know if I've gotten my shit properly piled up, so to speak," I grinned. "And I'm not sure he'll want me. I might just go visit an old friend in Boulder... lay low for awhile."

He nodded, staring out toward the road. "Did you get what you were after?" I thought about it a moment and felt myself smile.

"Some of it, at least," I said. He cleared his throat.

"Well, I'd sure like to take you out for a nice steak," he said without looking at me. I grinned.

"As long as I can buy dessert," I stuck out my hand, "I'm in." I could see him blushing a little, more in his mannerisms than in his skin and it softened my heart. "I'll meet you there around 6:30?" He nodded.

"Well, best get back to the shop. Always another napkin that needs drawn on." My giggle caught in my throat, touched by the tenderness in his statement, and the reminder that this calloused man had found a sweet, gentle expression. I could not hug him without a tear at the moment, and gave him a peace sign instead.

I spent the day in the park and walked back to the hotel as dusk settled on the naked trees. I indulged in a longer than normal shower, and put on mascara before I left for the restaurant. "I'm not going to let you get me drunk this time," I joked as he held the door open for me. He chuckled, more relaxed than usual. I was too. I knew it was because we both knew this was the end. We would walk away from each other in a couple of hours as friends that would never know each other again. We would expire, and that was just fine.

"Ummmm, I guess I'll take the Cabernet." I told the beautiful woman who stood at our table. "Wait. No... how about the Pino Gris? I'm sorry. I just don't know what I want tonight." I grinned when I looked at her, more at my ridiculous self than out of a need to practice proper etiquette. She accommodated me politely, but without a smile.

"So, Pino Gris, then?" she confirmed and I nodded.

"Sir?" she addressed him.

"Whiskey and water. Neat," David responded with a gruffness to his voice. I half smiled. He was covering up "shy" in front of this beautiful woman. She smiled stiffly at him, snapped her book closed and strode away.

"How was your day?" David asked after a short silence.

"Nice. I spent a lot of time in the park."

"You ready to go home to your boy yet?"

I gave him an inquisitive smile. "What's with you and 'my boy'?" He shifted uncomfortably for only a moment.

"Just wanna see that you are gonna be ok, is all."

I played defensive. "Oh, so you think I won't be ok out there in the world alone?" He nodded at the glass of wine our server set in front of me.

"I dunno. Will ya?" We both laughed. "I know you'll be fine. You're a tough kid. Just seems like you care about this guy and you're still holding him at arms length." I gave him a crooked grin.

"I'm shocked - albeit pleasantly - at your insight." We both took a sip to relieve the tension in the moment. I was a little defensive and I didn't know why. "The thing is, David, I just realized that all of my life I've been using something outside of myself.... a job or the love of a man or whatever... to make me happy. I've been defining myself as good, or valuable, or lovable because my boss appreciated me or the boyfriend I had was amazing. I don't want to be that woman. I want to live for ME. I want to love myself completely and just let "him" - whoever he is - be a compliment to my life, not a definition. I just don't know if I'm there yet."

David sat back in his chair, an amused smile on his face. "How many relationships you been in, Jaci?"

I got shy, but answered him anyway. "Oh, I don't know... 7, maybe."

"And who did the breaking up?"

Now I was confused. "I guess I did, mostly. Why?"

He nodded and twisted his glass to and fro on the table, taking forever to respond.

"My wife... Nancy... you remind me a lot of her..." he sipped his drink and curled his lips under at the bite of the whisky. "The way you talk, your strong personality, your damn independence." I grinned, and braced for battle.

"I think you get it. I bet your boyfriends adored you. I bet you let 'em do about anything they wanted." Now I was defensive for real.

"Within reason, yes. I did. I think people are responsible for their own lives, their own choices, their own happiness. So I let them do what they wanted and I did what I wanted. Well, you know, within reason." David looked at me.

"I don't know. I bet you did what they wanted, too."

"Well, of course," I started. He interrupted.

"I bet you *did* try to make them happy - by doing whatever you thought they wanted you to, even when you didn't really want to." I stared at him for a minute, embarrassed and shocked by the truth in what he was saying. "And then I bet you left because whether you knew it or not, you didn't want to be the person you were becoming." I was swirling my wine now, uncomfortable with the truth in his words.

"Doing what the other person wants is just what you do to show someone you love them, isn't it?" He shook his head without looking at me, and then looked me dead in the eye.

"No, that's what you do when you don't think the real you is good enough, and you've forgotten how to make yourself happy." He stared into his glass for a minute and then took another sip of his whisky neat. I downed an entire glass of water in an effort not to cry. Gratefully, I saw the waitress coming to take our orders and after she left I tried to turn the conversation.

"So, tell me more about Nancy." He looked at me a long time again, and then down.

"I loved her," he said into his drink before he looked back up at me. "She loved me too, I s'pect. Kept me at arms length though... felt like." I bristled at the implication.

"Why do you say that?"

"Oh, she'as always running off somewhere. 'Specially when she was mad at me. Whooooeee!" He gave a low whistle and chuckled. "She'd tell me I could do whatever I wanted to do, all sweet, and then just go get her bag and get in the car. Never knew where she was goin'." He stared past me. "Always came back though. Always."

"Maybe she just needed some time to herself," I said, defending us both.

He nodded. "I know she did." I fumbled around in my mind for what to say next and when I came up empty handed time and again, I took a sip of wine instead and munched the salad that had just been delivered.

Eventually the conversation turned to coffee, and art, and our mutual love of both things. I laughed around mouthfuls of perfectly cooked steak and his belly shook when he chuckled at me. He told me about Nancy's adventures... coming home with poison ivy in her most sensitive parts from squatting by a tree to pee, or with her hair braided up from a festival she'd been to. "She tried to work a comb through those damned dreadlocks for days 'for she let me just chop 'em off." We both laughed heartily. He told me about having to rescue her from a llama ranch not 45 miles from their house, just a half hour after she'd left one evening, because her car broke down. He towed her home and they spent the night drinking whiskey and wine in the backyard, and laughing about the whole thing.

He ordered us both a raspberry cheesecake because he said it was Nancy's favorite and the best raspberry cheesecake he'd ever had. "Real raspberries," he whispered loudly to me. "Lots of 'em. And homemade chocolate sauce." He was right. It was the best raspberry cheesecake I'd ever had. When I put $20 in the check jacket he snorted, pulled it out and shoved it back to me.

"That was the deal!" I protested. He scoffed. "That was just the deal to get you to come with me." He grinned. I knew I wouldn't win the argument and settled for a warm hug in thanks for his kindness.

We walked to the coffee shop to end the night with a cup. I told him it had better be decaf or I wouldn't sleep at all and he brought me wine instead. We sat out on the porch again, this time in the full dark of night sipping beer and wine and said nothing for a long while.

"Glad you spent a couple hours with this old man this week," he said without looking at me. "Was real nice. We don't get a lot of strangers 'round here. And none like you, li'l lady."

I grinned and took a sip. "I liked it too, David. It's nice to talk to someone about my crazy." He chuckled loudly. "But I'm nothing special. I'm just…"

He stopped smiling suddenly and interrupted me. "See? There you go again. Just like Nancy." He stood up abruptly and stared out into the night. "That woman never could believe that I loved her. She refused to see the good in her that everybody else saw." He was almost angry now, and I wasn't sure if it was the whisky or the topic but I could hear it in his voice, high with emotion. "I'm gonna give you a piece of advice. You'd better figure this 'I'm not special' shit out or it's gonna wreck your life. You ARE special. Damn it! And your guy is going to be lucky to have you, if you let him."

"If he's still there," I said, almost under my breath.

"I've known you two days and I can already see you are funny and smart..." he said, ignoring my comment. "You're strong and independent and kind and more forgiving than anyone I've ever met." He rocked back a little, almost as though he was reeling from his rant. I sat silent and still, watching him in awe.

"David, I..." He shook his head and thew up his hand to silence me.

"Here's the thing sweetheart," he said, quietly after a long pause. "All the time Nancy and I were together... I got so mad at her sometimes. I remember thinking a couple of times that maybe we shouldn't've gotten married. But now that she's gone, I don't remember why. Now that she's gone, all I can remember are the good things. Wish I'da spent more time payin' mind to that stuff when she was here."

My heart warmed. I nodded, afraid if I said something it would ruin the whole thing. He swirled the last of his beer and drank it, then took the bottle inside. A skittish little tabby cat was darting down the sidewalk after a leaf and I held as still as possible as he approached the steps. He looked warily at me but after a couple vocalizations of his displeasure at my presence, he began to climb the stairs pensively.

"Stinker! There you are." David let the screen door slam shut behind him and bent over, inviting the tabby to run to him. The little cat did exactly that and wove himself through David's legs for a full minute before he sat, tail twitching, and looked up at him. "Squirreliest little creature I ever saw," David said, shaking his head and grinning. "I swear he must have several of us old widowers he calls on." David went back into the shop and brought a shallow dish full of cream. Stinker lapped it up contentedly.

My eyes were getting heavy, the stars blurring, so I collected my bag, carried my glass inside, and bid the two bachelors on the porch a good morning - it was well after midnight. I told David I would be in for one last cup before I headed out of town, and hugged him whispering "thanks" in his ear before I pulled away. I scratched Stinker behind his ears, much to his dismay, and headed down the street with my sandals in my hand.

***

The next morning I sat in my car, letting the engine warm away the cold of several fall nights in the mountains, and watched the people of Miles City mill about on their way to the weekend. Some carried mugs of what I assumed to be coffee into storefronts, turning the open signs as they closed the door behind them, others took their place in the short line of cars headed - I presumed - to the next town over to work. I waited a few moments longer, drove to the top of the hill and parked in front of David's shop. There were several customers in line already and by the time I placed my order, there were several in line behind me. When David delivered my coffee I looked at him for as long a moment as I thought he could spare, and thanked him. "Figures," he said, gesturing to the line. I grinned, hugged him and left.

Pulling out of town my heart ached. I liked David. I liked the way he saw me. I would miss him. I would miss feeling like I did in front of him. He was right, of course, and I'd spent the whole walk back to the hotel last night thinking about it. I *had* tried to be what the men in my life wanted me to be because I didn't believe the me I was, was good enough. Then every time I left them and set out on my own again I had tried to find a place or a definition that would make me valuable, give me something to love about myself, and when I didn't find it, I fell back into another relationship and started the whole mess over again. In the process I'd given a child up for adoption, been divorced... hell, I hadn't even been able to take care of my first dog.

What a screw up I was! The guilt and embarrassment only lasted a moment longer than the thought though. *Damn*

162

it, no. You know what? There was good in those experiences too... And having the baby wasn't a "screw up"... who am I to say that it wasn't meant to happen that way. Maybe the world needed the little soul Charlie and I created and the baby needed the parents Charlie and I couldn't be. Maybe he will be particularly strong, or spiritual, or loving because of those circumstances.

He *was* an incredible little person. I knew because his parents wrote to me every year. They gave him the kind of life I would have wanted him to have and couldn't provide. *Maybe they needed his little piece of God in their lives.*

Same thing with the puppy. Maybe I had just been the vehicle to perfectly match the dog to the family she was meant for. Who was I to assume to know otherwise? I sent out a blessing of love and light to the dog and the boy and their families and took a deep breath. If I believed God was in my heart and I had followed my heart, I had done the right thing. I had to let that be true.

I took another deep breath. *Boulder does sound nice*, I thought. I could bring a very belated thank you gift to my friend's family for housing me all those years ago. I thought wistfully about going home, taking David's advice and letting Nichola 'in'. I knew I couldn't though, not yet.

Here I was again, running away from another relationship. Not because I didn't like who I was becoming, but this time, because I did - and I still wasn't enough.

Nichola loved to bike and ski... When we first met, he'd raced me home one night - my sister and I in my car, and he on his bicycle. Granted, it was downhill, but he'd almost beaten us. Biking was his primary form of transportation and he was incredibly good at it. I'd been so proud to show him my shiny new Kona. And when he'd given me a tour of his parents house, I'd been secretly thrilled to see the skis he'd ridden most of his childhood leaned up in a corner of the storage room downstairs. Even more so when he told me he still loved the sport and spent most winter weekends on my beloved Terry Peak. His mother had been far more verbal than he had in her excitement over the fact that we shared motorcycle riding too... he'd been riding dirt bikes since he was a kid, even borrowing his older sister's Harley once in awhile.

I hadn't needed to "become" anything at all with Nichola. We already shared a lot of things. I already was a biker and rider and skier...

Wait. Yeah! I was stunned by the realization and felt my heart flutter in my chest. I WAS a biker, a rider, a skier. The activities themselves didn't make me special, but the love I had for them kind of did. It made me the kind of person I had wanted to be. Or, at least, a version of that.

Maybe I am a little bit outdoorsy... a little bit adventurous, I thought, somewhat surprised at the perspective. Now that I thought about it, I supposed David might have been right as well. Maybe I could be considered a little bit independent. I was spiritual too, I supposed... I had a perspective on the Universe that I deeply, passionately believed in. I was even a little creative; I loved to paint and write. I was kind, most of the time. I loved easily.

I was sure I felt my heart swell with understanding. Those things were true. I *was* those things. And they were exactly the things I had wanted to be. David was the reflection, the appreciation, of the person I wanted to be - the person I was. It - I - had been there all along. I'd just been focusing on everything else. I had let the negative things rule my mind and eventually that was all I could see. But it wasn't all that was there. There were things I could love about me - even my scarred legs. I just had to start 'payin' mind' to the good... in me.

If I could train my brain to overcome fear, I could train it to see my own beauty and value. And really, that's all the amazing women that flocked around Nichola had, the women I so admired... they knew they were worth loving. That was all I needed to hold a man, a love, deep in my heart; know that it was possible for them to love me that much. The real me. The woman that made mistakes and thought herself nuts, but who was kind and passionate and adventurous and independent. All I had to do was see myself the way David saw me.

By the time I saw the sign for Belle Fourche, South Dakota, I knew I'd gotten what I needed. All of it. The lesson had been there on my motorcycle all along... it was all in my mind, and the most beautiful thing about my mind was that I could change it. I could focus on whatever I wanted and make my brain see what I wanted it to - the happy. No, I would never be beautiful, not like models in magazines. But I could love my body because I was damn lucky just to have it. And David was right - I was special - because I was the unique combination of things that I had wanted to be. The things I WAS. The ME I was.

***

It would have been snowing if there had been a drop of moisture in the air when I crossed the South Dakota line. The numbers on the gas pump clicked by and I let my breath cloud my face. When the filler gun finally clicked off I screwed the cap on my last tank of gas and climbed back into my car. Home was less than a half-hour away. I was excited. I had a plan, for the first time and it had nothing to do with a move, or a job, or a man.

I would simply love myself - and the container I was in - and that was all that would ever really matter. The rest would come from really knowing who I was, making decisions from my heart, and loving the life I was living.

The bitter wind could do nothing to dampen my spirits as I hauled my duffel bag up the narrow stairs. I left the television off and sat sipping tea, staring out the window at steam rising all over the city. I was home.

Jaclyn Lanae

SEVENTEEN

Snow was falling gently when I made the trek downtown to the little bar and concert venue where my favorite local bluegrass band was playing. The city looked soft through the swirling flakes, dancing lights strung across the street for the coming holiday. I could hear the music even before I rounded the corner and I smiled. I hoped Nichola would be there. I'd heard he'd moved his tarp into a friend's spare room while I was gone. I hadn't told him I was home because I wasn't sure what to say.

I felt good, really good for the first time in my adult life. My skin had cleared, almost magically over the past few weeks, and I had discovered it was easy to quit smoking when I finally loved myself and my body enough to want to take care of it.

Most of the tables were full when I walked through the door, pulling off my hat and shaking the cold into the air. I recognized a few friends and we hugged and laughed before I took my place in line. The house wine was more dry than I remembered but I ordered a full glass anyway and when I turned around I nearly spilled it's contents down the front of a brown plaid shirt. There was hurt in Nichola's eyes when I looked up at him, but he smiled and embraced me anyway.

"Good to see you," he said. My face was hot, flushed red with excitement and embarrassment. "Good to see you too! I wanted to call, but..." I looked around for a place to sit instead of finishing my sentence. I invited him with a glance and gestured to the only empty table in the room, awkwardly insulated by dart boards and a popcorn machine. He nodded almost imperceptibly.

I smiled and took a seat. He got right to the point as I took my first sip.

"Why'd you go?" he asked.

I looked out across the room at tables full of people chattering away or dancing in the tiny space in front of the band. "Oh..." I stalled, trying to put just the right words to a situation I still didn't fully understand. "I guess on some level I knew I wasn't really whole yet, and that if I were to keep dating you, I'd get distracted by 'us' and stop working on me." I didn't look at him but could sense he was nodding, looking down into his palms. "I think people sometimes put too much pressure on their partners or whatever to make them feel good, and important, and happy... and I didn't want to do that to you. I needed to figure out how to do it for myself." He glanced at me, then out toward the dance floor and back into my face.

"Did you get what you needed?" he asked as we clapped for the song.

I grinned, remembering my trip home. "Yeah, I did. I realized all the crazy stuff I was thinking was just that - thoughts. I was making myself broken and sad when I could have just as easily been making myself whole and happy. I just had to change my mind."

He looked at me feigning skepticism, but said nothing. When the banjo's voice could be heard again he grinned at me and I could have melted in his gaze. "Wanna dance?"

The Me I Was

The Me I Was

Authors Note:

This is a true story. I am, at heart, a writer and in order to facilitate a cohesive, entertaining narrative, certain details of this tale were pieced together with the limited memory and perspective of several people involved. As is often true with memories, time and individual filters can color perspective. This is an accepted truth in communication of all kinds, and must be an accepted truth in our lives.

Many, many people were involved in my survival, in my care, in my life. Many of them have their own stories to tell, incredible tales of bravery, determination, and triumph, regardless of their relationship to me or to the experience we shared. I have not included those stories here because I could never accurately tell those stories, and more importantly, they are not my stories to tell.

While I have changed the names of the beautiful souls involved in this part of my life, their presence was very real and I am deeply grateful for the role each and every one of them have played. I believe we draw to ourselves the people we need, to teach us, lead us, and support us. I am so blessed to have attracted so many beautiful beings.

There were a lot of people who contributed greatly to my survival, my recovery, and my success in completing this book. While I could never thank them all appropriately, I will attempt some semblance of offering credit for their contributions here. This list likely means nothing to most, but it is very likely we all have a list much like this.

Jaclyn Lanae

The Me I Was

My deepest gratitude...

To the people on the scene of the accident, and the doctors, nurses, and hospital staff, who did not give up on me.

To my family, who fought for me, cared for me, and suffered silently at my side, sometimes far more than I.

To my friends, who treated me as though nothing was wrong, and let me talk about it when something was.

To the people far and wide who prayed for me… the priests and churches and families all across the United States and even Europe who sent thoughts of love and light, grace and healing to a woman most of them had never met.

To the staff and owners of Black Hills Harley-Davidson®, and to the entire motorcycle community who prayed for me, visited me, and donated all they could to help me pay for my medical expenses and get me back on my feet.

To the friends and family who encouraged me to write this book, believed in my ability to do so, supported me while I did it, proofed and edited and proofed again, and then donated money to help me pay for the first beautiful box of them.

To the strangers who hold this book in their hands…

Thank you.

To Trevor. We got a second chance. Live it to the fullest, baby.

Jaclyn Lanae

If you enjoyed this book, please consider letting the world know on Amazon.com or Goodreads.com. Rate the book, leave a comment, or both.

To connect with Ms. Lanae in the digital world, follow her on Goodreads, Twitter, Pinterest, or Facebook.

Ms. Lanae invites the opportunity to speak on a variety of topics. If you would like to book an engagement, or have other questions, comments, or feedback, please contact her at www.AuthorJLanae.com.

Jaclyn Lanae

Shelter50 Publishing Collective
Giving voice to revolutionary ideas and stories

The Shelter50 Publishing Collective exists for the possibility of giving voice to authors with culturally subversive and revolutionary ideas and stories. Our hope is to put to print books with the potential to transform people and communities in an effort to leave the world in better condition than we were handed it.

www.Shelter50PublishingCollective.com

@Shelter50Books

Jaclyn Lanae

The Me I Was

22492875R00117

Made in the USA
Columbia, SC
01 August 2018